SECOND EDITION

Super Practice Book

4

Garan Holcombe

CAMBRIDGE
UNIVERSITY PRESS

Map of the Book

Simple Present Questions

Does Polly **like** going to the movie theater?

Yes, she does. She goes every week!

Use **present simple** questions to ask people about habits and routines. Yes/No questions are formed with **be** or **do**:

Are you from Izmir?	Yes, I am.	No, I'm not.
Are we / they from Istanbul?	Yes, we / they are.	No, we / they aren't.
Is he / she from Bursa?	Yes, he / she is.	No, he / she isn't.
Do you / we / they like playing the guitar?	Yes, I / we / they do.	No, I / we / they don't.
Does he / she love watching movies?	Yes, he / she does.	No, he / she doesn't.

"Wh" questions are formed by putting **where**, **what**, **why**, etc., before **be** or **do**:

What is your favorite type of music?

1 Complete the questions with either *do / does* or the correct form of *be*.

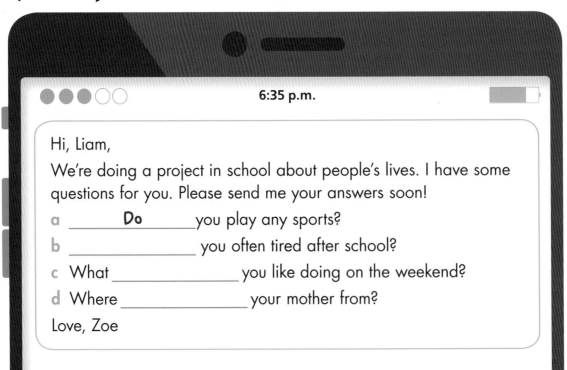

6:35 p.m.

Hi, Liam,

We're doing a project in school about people's lives. I have some questions for you. Please send me your answers soon!

a _____**Do**_____ you play any sports?

b _____ you often tired after school?

c What _____ you like doing on the weekend?

d Where _____ your mother from?

Love, Zoe

2 Match the questions from Activity 1 with the answers below.

```
●●●○○                          7:05 p.m.

Hi, Zoe,

Thanks for your questions! Here are my answers.

1  Yes, I am. I often feel very sleepy in the evening.        [ b ]

2  Lots of things! I go running with my brother. I watch movies. Oh, I draw, too.
   I love drawing!                                            [  ]

3  China. I always speak Mandarin with her. I love it!       [  ]

4  Yes, I do. I swim three times a week, and I play basketball on Sunday mornings. [  ]

Good luck with your project!

Love, Liam
```

3 Complete the dialogue with the words from the box.

does ~~what~~ don't who live Yes

Mehmet	**(1)** _____**What**_____	does your brother do, Nick?
Nick	He's a journalist.	
Mehmet	Really? Is it an exciting job?	
Nick	I **(2)** _____ know. I think he likes it.	
Mehmet	**(3)** _____ does he work for?	
Nick	He writes for *El País* newspaper. In Spain.	
Mehmet	What **(4)** _____ he write about?	
Nick	He interviews famous people: actors and singers.	
Mehmet	Does he **(5)** _____ in Madrid?	
Nick	**(6)** _____, he does. In a place called La Latina.	

Simple Past Questions

Did you **have** a good time at the party, Petra? **Was** the food good?

Language Focus

Use **simple past questions** to ask what people did at a specific time in the past.

Yes/No questions are formed with **was / were** or **did**:

Were you at the park yesterday?   Yes, I was.   No, I wasn't.

Was he / she in the movie theater?   Yes, he / she was.   No, he / she wasn't.

The question form with **did** is the same for every person, i.e., **I**, **he**, **she**, **they**:

Did you / he / she / we / they go surfing?

"Wh" questions are formed by putting **Where**, **What**, **Why**, etc., before **was / were** and **did**:

Where were you on Saturday?   **Where** did you go on vacation?

1 Complete the questions and answers about a vacation in Italy.

1 __Were__ you happy on vacation?

Yes, we __were__.

2 _____ your brother with you?

No, he _____. He had to work.

3 _____ you go to Venice?

No, we _____. We went to Rome.

4 _____ your parents like Italy?

Yes, they _____.
They want to go back next year!

5 _____ the people friendly?

Yes, they _____.
They taught me some Italian.

2 Are the questions correct or incorrect? Correct the questions you think are incorrect.

1 What do you do yesterday?
   Incorrect.   What did you do yesterday?

2 Were you at school yesterday?
   _____   _____

3 Do you go to the beach last summer?
   _____   _____

4 Was you tired this morning?
   _____   _____

5 What was the last movie you saw?
   _____   _____

6 Do you did your homework last night?
   _____   _____

3 Answer the questions from Activity 2.

1 _____
  _____

2 _____
  _____

3 _____
  _____

4 _____
  _____

5 _____
  _____

6 _____
  _____

Reading: A Poem

1 Read the poem, then put questions a–f in the correct order.

The Questioner

Do you like your school, your house, your life?
Do you eat your food with a fork and knife?
Do you have adventures big and small?
Do you think of yesterday at all?
When you were young,
What did you do?

Did you go on bumper cars bright and new?
Were the roller coasters white and blue?
In traffic circles, without a care,
Did the boys and girls have golden hair?
Are you different now
You know much more?
Or are you the same as you were before?

The simple past is present now,
The moments come and go, and how!
We go on asking questions, yes,
But what's the last one?
Can you guess?

a When you were young, what did you do? ☐

b Are you different now? ☐

c Were roller coasters white and blue? ☐

d Do you like your school, your house, your life? **1**

e What's the last one? ☐

f Do you have adventures big and small? ☐

1 **Match the words with the definitions.**

1 rhythm

2 rhyme

3 verse

4 poet

5 poem

a This is writing with short sentences (called lines) and using words that often rhyme.

b This is someone who writes poems.

c This is when the ends of two words have the same sound, e.g., *dog / log, blue / do, door / floor.*

d This is how the words sound together.

e This is a group of lines that forms part of a poem. "The Questioner" has three of these.

Help with Writing

Poems are not easy to write in another language. Think of words that rhyme, e.g., *fat, hat, cat, mat.* Then try writing a simple poem with a simple rhythm, e.g., *My dog is fat, he wears a hat, he hates the cat, she chews his mat.*

2 **Complete the poem with the words from the box.**

~~me~~   Jo   floors   low

The Treasure Hunt

"Where is the gold, the gold?" said Lee.

"What gold? What gold?" said Tom to (1) _____ me _____.

I did not know, so turned to go,

And talked to Sue and Mark and (2) _____.

We looked at maps, for clues and doors,

And holes in walls and wooden (3) _____.

We looked up high, we looked down (4) _____,

Until it was our time to go.

3 **Now write another verse for the poem. Follow the rhythm of the verses.**

_____

_____

_____

Listening: Adventures

1 🎧 **01** Listen and check ☑ or put an X ☒.

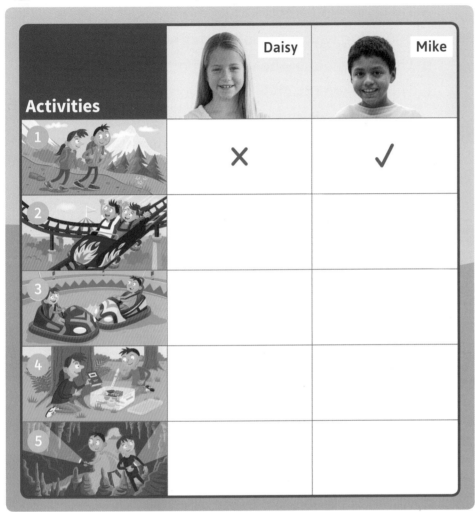

Activities	Daisy	Mike
1	✗	✓
2		
3		
4		
5		

2 🎧 **02** Listen to Jacob talk about his adventure. Circle the correct answers.

1 Which mountain did Jacob climb?
  (a) Cave Mountain.
  b Castle Mountain.

2 How did he get to the mountain?
  a By train.
  b By car.

3 Who did he go with?
  a His parents and his brother.
  b His parents.

4 What did Jacob think of the climb?
  a It was fun, but it was dangerous too.
  b It was dangerous, and it wasn't fun.

5 How long did Jacob hike for?
  a Two hours.
  b Four hours.

6 Which mountain does Jacob want to climb next?
  a Diamond Mountain.
  b Treasure Mountain.

1 **Look and write. Then play the *You Can …, Too* game.**

> What's Number 2?

> Go on a Ferris wheel. You can go on a roller coaster, too!

d **rive** ____
b ____ ____

g ____ on a
F ____ ____

r ____ a b ____

f ____ a k ____

c ____ a m ____

w ____ on the
b ____

2 **Work with a friend. Talk about the things to do in Activity 1.**

> Do you like going on a Ferris wheel?

> No, I don't. It's scares me! What about you?

> I love going on a Ferris wheel. It's exciting!

3 **With your friend, imagine you went on an adventure yesterday. What did you do? Think of four activities. Then talk about your adventure.**

> Yesterday, Tom and I went on an adventure. We went to a castle at the top of a mountain. We rode our bikes to get to the mountain, and we climbed the mountain to get to the castle. We looked for treasure in the castle, and we found a statue!

1 Have To / Am Not Allowed To

You **are not allowed to take** photographs of the paintings, and you **have to turn off** your phones.

Language Focus

Use **have to** to talk about what it is necessary to do, e.g., I **have to** buy my mother a birthday card.

Use **am not allowed to** to tell someone not to do something, e.g., You **aren't allowed to** play the drums so loudly.

1 **Read what Maria says, then circle the correct verbs to complete the sentences.**

"Mom and Dad say I don't do enough to help them with the chores. I'm going to show them how much I can do. To help me, I have a list of things I have to do and things I am not allowed to do. I'm going to put it on my wall in my room …"

1 I (have to) / am not allowed to clean my room at least once a month.

2 I have to / am not allowed to leave my clothes on the floor.

3 I have to / am not allowed to do the dishes on weekends.

4 I have to / am not allowed to help Dad in the yard on Sunday afternoons.

5 I have to / am not allowed to help Mom wash her car once a month.

6 I have to / am not allowed to put dirty plates on the floor.

2 Complete the story with the verbs from the box.

clean ~~wear~~ be learn toast use

The Never-ending Orders of
Old King Marvin

Old King Marvin lived in a huge castle near Learnum Wood. His favorite thing was telling people what to do. "You are not allowed to (1) __wear__ your crown in the yard," he said every morning to Good Queen Tess. "It might fall off."

A handsome young knight named Gordon the Magnificent lived in the castle, too. "You have to (2) _____ your shield and helmet," Old King Marvin said to Gordon. "And you have to (3) _____ how to use your sword. But you are not allowed to (4) _____ it inside the castle."

One morning, Old King Marvin went to the kitchen. "I would like to make breakfast this morning," he said to the cook. "Is that all right?" "Yes, sir," said the cook. Ten minutes later, Good Queen Tess heard a loud voice in the kitchen. "I'm very sorry, sir, but you have to (5) _____ the bread for thirty-three seconds longer. You have to (6) _____ careful with bread. It's easy to get it wrong." Good Queen Tess smiled to herself, happy to hear someone telling her husband what to do for a change.

3 Look at the pictures. Complete the sentences using *have to* and *am not allowed to*.

The Newbury Park Rules

1 You **'re not allowed to climb** the trees.

2 You _____ your trash in the trash can.

3 You _____ on the flowers.

4 You _____ your dog on a leash.

5 You _____ in the lake.

6 You _____ the ducks.

Direct and Indirect Objects

Juanita, give **him the ball**, please.

Language Focus

Use **direct and indirect objects** to talk about things or people affected by the action of the verb.

Subject	Verb	Indirect object	Direct object
Jeremy	gave	David	the book.
I	made	my sister	a sandwich.
Don't	show	me	the answer.

The direct object is the person or thing affected by the action of the verb. It answers the question **what**, e.g., *What did Jeremy give to David?*

The indirect object is also the person or thing affected by the action of the verb; it answers the question **who**, e.g., *Who did Jeremy give the book to?*

We sometimes put the indirect object at the end of the sentence, where it usually follows the prepositions **to** and **for**.

*Jeremy gave the book **to David**.*   *Don't show the answer **to me**.*

*I made a sandwich **for my sister**.*

1 Replace the underlined words with object pronouns.

1 My brother and I gave <u>a necklace</u> to <u>Mel</u>.   My brother and I gave it to her.

2 She gave <u>the book</u> to <u>Stan and Toni</u>. _____

3 They gave <u>the book</u> to <u>Tim</u>. _____

4 He gave <u>the book</u> to <u>his mother</u>. _____

5 She gave <u>the book</u> to <u>my father</u>. _____

6 He gave <u>the book</u> to <u>my brother and me</u>. _____

2 Rewrite the sentences with the words in the correct order.

1 Show / the bracelet, / me / please / .   <u>Show me the bracelet, please.</u>

2 Don't / the story / to / tell / Juan / .   _____

3 You have to / the dress / buy / Gabriella / for / .   _____

4 I gave / the belt / Wang Li / to / .   _____

5 I bought / Sheila / for / a hat / .   _____

6 Sarah / me / gave / the necklace / .   _____

3 Complete the story with the pronouns *it*, *her*, *them*, *us*, and *me*.

Mr. James and the Bag of Candy

"Give (1) <u>**them**</u> to (2) _____, please," said Mr. James.

"But the candy is Sandra's, Mr. James," said Sonny.

"Yes, I know the candy is Sandra's, but don't give (3) _____ back to (4) _____. It's not recess. You know the rule."

"Yes, Mr. James, I know (5) _____; you remind (6) _____ all every day. We aren't allowed to eat candy in class."

"Anything," said Mr. James. "You aren't allowed to eat anything in class. Come on. Sandra can have (7) _____ back at recess."

I gave Mr. James the bag of candy and sat in my chair. Five minutes later, I looked up from my math book.

"Mr. James!" I said. "You're eating (8) _____. But you said …"

"Yes, I know I did, Sonny," said Mr. James, smiling, "but it is very good candy."

Reading: A Postcard

1 Read the postcard, then answer the questions.

Dear Eve,

Yesterday, we went to the fantastic Chocolate Museum. You have to go there!

A guide told us all about the history of chocolate, and we watched a short movie about how to make chocolate. Dad thought the movie was great. They had a fantastic collection of old chocolate wrappers, too. Grandma really liked that.

They also gave us some free chocolate to take home. It was delicious!

I hope you are well.

Love,
Li Yan

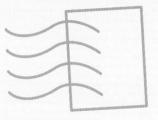

Eve Blackburn

23 January Street

Belfast

Northern Ireland

BT9 5AB

1 Where did Li Yan and her family go?

They went to the Chocolate Museum.

2 What did the guide tell them about?

3 Who thought the movie was very good?

4 Who liked the collection of old chocolate wrappers?

5 What did they get to take home?

1 Complete the descriptions of the museums with *have to* or *am not allowed to*.

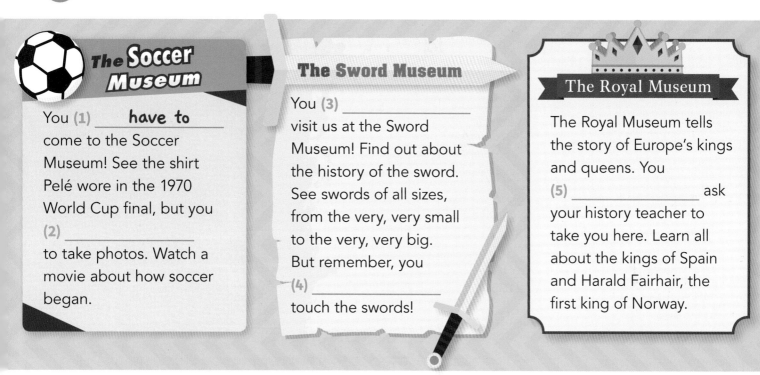

The Soccer Museum

You **(1)** ___ have to ___ come to the Soccer Museum! See the shirt Pelé wore in the 1970 World Cup final, but you **(2)** _____ to take photos. Watch a movie about how soccer began.

The Sword Museum

You **(3)** _____ visit us at the Sword Museum! Find out about the history of the sword. See swords of all sizes, from the very, very small to the very, very big. But remember, you **(4)** _____ touch the swords!

The Royal Museum

The Royal Museum tells the story of Europe's kings and queens. You **(5)** _____ ask your history teacher to take you here. Learn all about the kings of Spain and Harald Fairhair, the first king of Norway.

Help with Writing

We usually write postcards to describe our experiences to friends and family. We often use adjectives such as *excellent*, *great,* and *fantastic* to talk about what we did.

2 Imagine you went to one of the museums in Activity 1. Write a postcard to tell a friend about it. Use Li Yan's postcard on the Reading page to help you.

Listening: Exhibits

1 🎧 **03** Listen and write *t* (true) or *f* (false).

Rules at the Shield Museum

1 You have to show your ticket to the woman at the door. **[t]**
2 You can touch some of the shields. ☐
3 You aren't allowed to take photos of the shields. ☐
4 You have to carry your bag inside the museum. ☐
5 You can see some shields of famous kings. ☐
6 You have to leave at five o'clock. ☐

2 🎧 **04** Listen to Kasim's story. Complete each sentence with one word.

1 Kasim and his class visited the Knight ___Museum___ yesterday.
2 Kasim's friend William took a _____ from a shelf and put it on.
3 At the museum, you aren't allowed to touch the helmets, shields, or _____ .
4 The woman wasn't happy with Mr. Martin because he _____ in the museum.
5 After the problems, the children didn't touch things, run, or _____ .
6 William doesn't want to be a _____ in the school play.

1 Look and write. Then play the description game.

> A knight uses this to fight with.

> It's a sword!

crown

Help with Speaking

Some words have silent letters. The words *sword* and *knight* have silent letters: you don't pronounce the *w* in *sword* and the *k* and *gh* in *knight*.

2 Work with a friend. Read and talk about the museum rules.

The Museum of Queens and Kings

Remember ...

1 You have to show your ticket at the door.

2 You have to put your bag in a locker.

3 You aren't allowed to take photos of the exhibits.

4 You aren't allowed to use your phone.

5 You aren't allowed to run or shout.

3 With your friend, write three "dream rules" for the museum in Activity 2. Then talk about your rules.

> You have to touch the crowns and bracelets. You can put them on and have fun! You aren't allowed to leave until you wear your favorite queen or king costume.

Dream Rules for the Museum of Queens and Kings

You have to _____.

You can _____.

You _____.

2 Connectors

We stayed in a nice town, **and** we went swimming every day. Lola didn't swim **because** the water was really cold!

Language Focus

And, **but**, **so**, and **because** are **connectors**. Use them to join two parts of a sentence.

Use **and** and **but** to connect two ideas. Use **but** when the second idea is different from the first. Use a comma before them.

*We had picnics in the fields, **and** we walked through the forest.*
*I liked having picnics, **but** I didn't like walking through the forest*

Use **because** and **so** to talk about the reasons for an action. Use a comma before **so**.

*I was tired, **so** I went home.*   *I went home **because** I was tired.*

1 **Circle the correct connectors to complete the sentences.**

1 We went to the town, _____ we climbed the mountain.

   a so   b (and)   c but

2 We walked by the river, _____ we didn't swim in it.

   a but   b because   c and

3 We wanted to go on the river, _____ we took a boat to the island.

   a but   b and   c so

4 We went back to the town early _____ Mom was sleepy.

   a because   b and   c so

2 Complete the poem with *and*, *so*, *but*, or *because*.

The Park Poem

It was a beautiful day,

(1) _____**So**_____ we all went to play.

We laughed, (2) _____ we joked a lot.

We sat in the shade

Of a towering tree

(3) _____ we were hungry and hot.

After sandwiches, chocolate,

Bananas, and more,

We were sleepy, (4) _____ then Ricky said,

"I don't know about you,

My two favorite friends,

(5) _____ I think I'm ready for bed."

3 Complete the sentences with your own ideas.

My Weekend

On Friday, I did my homework, and (1) ___**I had dinner**___. I didn't go to the movie

theater because (2) _____. On Saturday morning, I was really hungry,

so (3) _____. On Saturday afternoon, I went to Dominic's birthday party,

but (4) _____. On Sunday morning, it was sunny, so (5) _____.

I usually go to my grandparents' house on Sunday afternoons, but last Sunday

(6) _____ because _____. On Sunday evening, I watched

TV and (7) _____. I went to bed early because (8) _____.

Could / Couldn't

What **could** you **do** when you were young, Grandma?

Oh, I **could do** lots of things, my dear. I **could walk** for hours, but not get tired. I **could run**, I **could swim**, and I **could go** ice skating. And these days, I can do jigsaw puzzles. There, that's the final piece!

Language Focus

Use **could** / **couldn't** to talk about abilities you had or didn't have in the past.

*When she was a girl, she **couldn't** swim, but she **could** ride a bike.*

Yes/No questions are formed in the following way:

Could *you / he / she / we / they make pancakes?*

*Yes, I / he / she / we / they **could**.*

*No, I / he / she / we / they **couldn't**.*

1 Answer the questions with *Yes, I could* or *No, I couldn't.*

1 Could you walk when you were six months old?   No, I couldn't.

2 Could you speak when you were one year old? _____

3 Could you run when you were three years old? _____

4 Could you catch a ball when you were four years old? _____

5 Could you read when you were five years old? _____

6 Could you write when you were seven years old? _____

2 Complete the questions with the verbs from the box.

speak   play   climb   ~~run~~   ski   ride

www.theoldpeopleswebsite.com

The **Old People's** Website

When you were a young man …

1 could you ___**run**___ fast?

2 could you _____ mountains?

3 could you _____ any other languages?

4 could you _____ the guitar?

5 could you _____ a motorcycle?

6 could you _____ or snowboard?

3 Match the questions in Activity 2 with the answers.

a No, I couldn't, but my brother could. He was a member of a club. He went up Everest once! ☐ 2

b Yes, I could. I didn't like driving cars, but I loved my second-hand Harley-Davidson! ☐

c No, I couldn't. I didn't go on winter vacations. They were too expensive! ☐

d No, I couldn't. I could play the violin, but I didn't learn to play anything else. ☐

e Yes, I could. I lived in Buenos Aires for five years when I was in my twenties, so my Spanish was very good. ☐

f Yes, I could. I loved doing that. I used to run by the river near my house every morning. ☐

Reading: A Story

1   **Read the story. Then complete the summary with the words from the box.**

The Strange Tale of
Jim Garry's Mountain

It was the mayor who saw it first. "Another beautiful morning," he said to himself as he opened his curtains. "Wait a minute. Jim Garry's Mountain is …"

It was all the people could talk about. "How can we climb it now?" they asked. Everyone was very worried, so they met at the Town Hall that evening to discuss the problem. "Thank you all for coming," said the mayor. "Now as you know, Jim Garry's mountain is …"

"It's not just Jim Garry's Mountain," said a voice.

An old man near the door stood up. His long hair and beard were gray.

"Excuse me," said the mayor, "this meeting is for the people of the town only."

"Don't you want to know what's happening? Why there is no water in the river and no grass in the fields?"

"What are you talking about? We are here to talk about where our mountain went."

"Everything is going because you don't take care of it. You have to take care of the world around you, Mayor. That is all I want to say. Good evening to you."

The people were more interested in who the man was than what he had to say. Nobody noticed that the forests, fields, lakes, and islands were not there any more. The only thing left in the town was the Town Hall and the people in it.

> mountain   Town Hall   mayor   people   ~~town~~   rivers

One morning, the mayor of the (1) __**town**__ finds that the (2) _____ is not there. The (3) _____ of the town are very worried. They have a meeting at the (4) _____. At the meeting, an old man that nobody knows says why everything is going from the town: the trees, the (5) _____, the lakes. The (6) _____ is not very happy with the old man. The old man leaves, and the people talk about him. They do not notice what is happening around them.

1 **Match the story types with the definitions.**

1 comedy
2 history
3 fantasy
4 romance
5 science fiction

a a story about something that happened in the past

b a story about things that aren't real or things that can't happen, e.g., a story in which people can fly

c a story that makes you laugh

d a story about technology, the future, and space

e a story about people who fall in love

Help with Writing

Try to make your readers interested in your story. One way to do that is to give them a question they want to find the answer to. For example, the opening sentence of "The Strange Tale of Jim Garry's Mountain" is "It was the mayor who saw it first." The writer doesn't tell us what "it" is, so we want to read on to find out.

2 **You are going to write a short story about something strange that happens in a town. You have to write it in the simple past. Before you write your story, plan it by making notes about the following:**

- the type of story (e.g., science fiction, fantasy)
- the characters
- the plot

3 **Now write your short story. Use "The Strange Tale of Jim Garry's Mountain" and your notes from Activity 2 to help you.**

Listening: Places

1 🎧 05 **Listen and put Ana's story in order.**

☐ They walked on a long path through a forest.

☐ Ana took lots of photos.

☐ It started to rain.

1 Last weekend, Ana went to the country with her parents.

☐ Ana and her parents had a picnic.

☐ They climbed up a mountain.

☐ Ana and her parents had cake in a café.

2 🎧 06 **What could Leo do when he was six? Listen and check ✓ or put an X ☒.**

1 Look at these places, and imagine you went there. Play the guessing game.

> I was in town. I wanted to look at comic books, so …

> You went to a bookstore! I was outdoors. I wanted to swim, so …

> You went to a lake!

bookstore

lake

café

movie theater

mountain

forest

2 Look at Activity 1, and choose a place that you went to. Write answers. Then practice.

1 Where did you go?

_____

2 Who did you go with?

_____

3 How did you get there?

_____

4 Why did you go there?

_____

5 What did you do and see?

_____

3 Talk about your place.

> Last weekend, I went to a lake with my family. We got there by train. We went there because we love being in the country. We walked around the lake, and then we swam in it. We saw some big fish and beautiful birds!

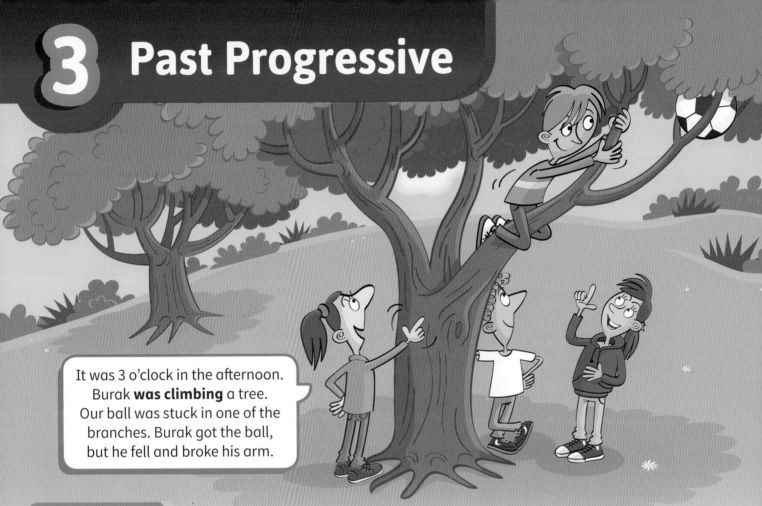

It was 3 o'clock in the afternoon. Burak **was climbing** a tree. Our ball was stuck in one of the branches. Burak got the ball, but he fell and broke his arm.

Language Focus

Use the **past progressive** to talk about events that were happening at a particular moment in the past, e.g., *Onur **was climbing** a mountain.*

Form the past progressive with **was** / **were** + **verb** + **ing**:

*I / he / she **was watching** a TV show about firefighters.*

*We / you / they **were playing** soccer in the yard.*

1 **Circle the correct verb forms to complete the text.**

On Saturday afternoon, everyone **(1)** (was) / were doing something. My brother Pablo **(2)** was / were reading about the Great Fire of London. My parents **(3)** was / were cleaning the kitchen. My sister Lucia **(4)** was / were playing a computer game called *Emergency!* My cousins Maria and Gonzalo **(5)** was / were painting. I **(6)** was / were doing something, too. Can you guess what it was? Yes, that's right! I **(7)** was / were watching what everyone else was doing!

2 Match 1–6 with a–f.

1 I was

2 My brother was

3 My grandparents were

4 My sisters were in

5 My dog was

6 Sarah, my best friend, was

a chasing the cat around the yard. That's her favorite thing to do.

b at home watching a TV show about emergency workers. Grandma said it was very interesting.

c making a web page on the internet. She's very good with technology.

d the kitchen, making their favorite type of pizza: bananas and onion. Ugh!

e sleeping. He's always tired. He works really hard in school.

f doing my science homework. I didn't enjoy doing it because it was really hard!

3 Correct the verbs in sentences 1–5. Make past progressive sentences.

1 The firefighters were climb the ladder.

   The firefighters were climbing the ladder.

2 The police officers were ran very quickly.

   _____

3 Sara was make a sandwich.

   _____

4 The paramedic were working very hard.

   _____

5 My friends was watching a movie about a flood.

   _____

4 Complete the sentences so they are true for you.

1 On Saturday morning, I _____.

2 On Saturday afternoon, my parents _____.

3 On Saturday evening, my family _____.

4 On Sunday morning, I _____.

5 On Sunday afternoon, my friends and I _____.

6 On Sunday evening, I _____.

Past Progressive Questions

What **was** Dad **doing** this morning?

He **was cleaning** the car. It was so dirty!

Language Focus

Use **past progressive questions** to ask someone what they were doing at a particular moment in the past, e.g.,

I called you at six. You didn't answer. Were you washing dishes?

Yes/No questions are formed with **was / were** + **verb** + **ing**, e.g.,

Were *we / they sleep***ing** *last night?*   *Yes, we / they were.*   *No, we / they weren't.*

Was *he / she do***ing** *his homework?*   *Yes, he / she was.*   *No, he / she wasn't.*

"Wh" questions are formed by putting **where**, **what**, **why**, etc., before **was** / **were** + **verb** + **ing**, e.g.

What *book* **were** *you* **reading**?   *I was reading one about history.*

Where were *your friends* **going**?   *They were going to the park to play tennis.*

1 Rewrite the questions with the words in the correct order.

1 you / were / what / yesterday / doing / ? <u>What were you doing yesterday?</u>

2 you / were / sleeping / ? _____

3 what / friend / doing / was / your / ? _____

4 was / book / she / reading / a / ? _____

5 going / you / were / where / ? _____

6 at / brother / three / doing / your / was / what / o'clock / ? _____

2 Complete the questions with *was / were* and the verbs from the box in the correct form. Then write the answers.

play   drink   read   run   sit   clean   ~~eat~~

1 ___Was___ the man in the blue T-shirt ___cleaning___ the window? **Yes, he was.**

2 _____ the man in the red T-shirt _____ pizza? _____

3 _____ the two women _____ water? _____

4 _____ the woman in the red dress _____ down? _____

5 _____ the police officer _____ after a man? _____

6 _____ the man with glasses _____ a book? _____

3 Complete the questions.

1 What / you / do / four o'clock / afternoon / Monday?
  __What were you doing at four o'clock in the afternoon on Monday?__

2 What / you / do / six o'clock / morning / Wednesday?

  _____

3 What / you / do / five o'clock / afternoon / Friday?

  _____

4 What / you / do / nine o'clock / evening / Saturday?

  _____

5 What / you / do / six o'clock / morning / Sunday?

  _____

Reading: An Email

1 Read the email, then answer the questions.

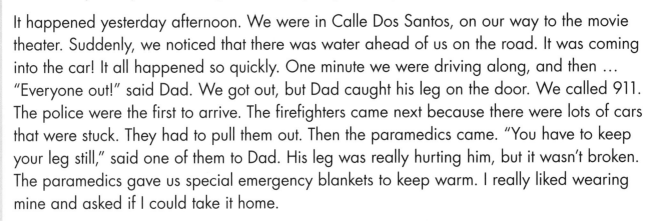

To grannyandgranpa@oldpeopleemail.com

Subject The Great Flood of Calle Dos Santos

Hi, Granny,

I have some news. We had an accident yesterday.
Don't worry, everyone is all right. Mom is going to call you later.

It happened yesterday afternoon. We were in Calle Dos Santos, on our way to the movie
theater. Suddenly, we noticed that there was water ahead of us on the road. It was coming
into the car! It all happened so quickly. One minute we were driving along, and then …
"Everyone out!" said Dad. We got out, but Dad caught his leg on the door. We called 911.
The police were the first to arrive. The firefighters came next because there were lots of cars
that were stuck. They had to pull them out. Then the paramedics came. "You have to keep
your leg still," said one of them to Dad. His leg was really hurting him, but it wasn't broken.
The paramedics gave us special emergency blankets to keep warm. I really liked wearing
mine and asked if I could take it home.

I have to go now, Granny. Dad can't walk very well right now, so he wants me to go
to the kitchen and make him a cup of tea.

Email soon with all your news!

Love,
Valentina

1 When did the accident happen? __It happened yesterday afternoon.__

2 Where were Valentina and her parents going? _____

3 What happened? _____

4 What did Valentina's dad hurt? _____

5 Who arrived after the police officers? _____

6 What did they give Valentina's family? _____

1 Write the phrases from the box in the correct part of the table.

> Bye for now,   Hi, _____ ,   Dear _____ ,
> Email me soon,   Best wishes,   How are you?
> Hello, _____ ,   Is everything OK?   How are things?

Starting an Email	
Asking How Someone Is	
Finishing an Email	

Help with Writing

When you tell someone your news in an email, give them the important information, but do not write too much.

2 You are going to write an email to Valentina telling her all about a fire in a local café. Before you write, make notes about the following:

- when and where the fire started
- what you were doing when it started
- what the firefighters said and did

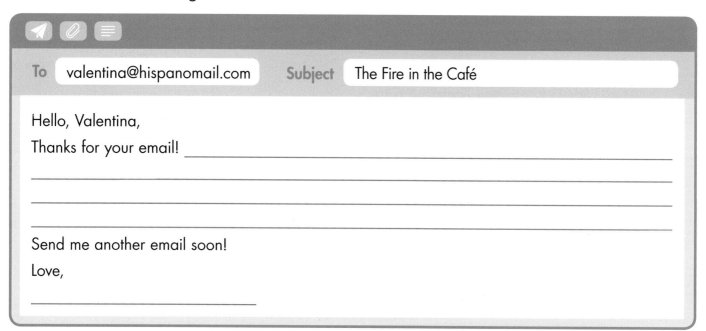

| To | valentina@hispanomail.com | Subject | The Fire in the Café |

Hello, Valentina,

Thanks for your email! _____

_____

_____

_____

Send me another email soon!

Love,

_____

Listening: Emergency, Emergency!

1 🎧 07 **Listen to Jack's story and write *t* (true) or *f* (false).**

1 Jack, Lea, and John went to a park last Sunday. `t`

2 They climbed the tallest tree in the park. ☐

3 The children got to the top of the tree, and it wasn't raining. ☐

4 There was a storm and a flood, so the children couldn't climb down the tree. ☐

5 Jack called his parents and 911. ☐

6 A firefighter helped the children come down from the tree. ☐

2 🎧 08 **Listen to the conversations. Circle the correct answers.**

1 What was Theo doing yesterday at three o'clock?

   a He was reading a book.   (b) He was watching a movie.

2 Was Amy watching TV yesterday at four o'clock?

   a Yes, she was.   b No, she wasn't.

3 How was Jamie yesterday?

   a He wasn't feeling well.   b He was feeling OK.

4 Who forgot to do the homework?

   a Eva.   b Harry.

5 What was Freddie doing before twelve o'clock yesterday?

   a He was sleeping.   b He was having breakfast.

6 Where was it raining this morning?

   a In the town near the beach.   b At the beach.

1 Work with a friend. Look at the pictures and tell the story. Use the words and the simple past and past progressive.

> Yesterday, it was a warm day. The sun was shining and …

warm day / sun shine / children do some work

fire alarm ring / fire

children and teacher go to playground / room at the top on fire

firefighters arrive / everything OK

2 Choose one of the photos. Imagine you are an emergency worker. How did you help the animal? Write answers. Then practice.

1 What's your job?

_____

2 What happened?

_____

3 What was the animal doing?

_____

4 How did you help the animal?

_____

3 Tell your story from Activity 2.

> I'm a police officer. Last Monday, it rained all day, and there was a flood. I was driving my police car and saw a dog on a roof. The dog was …

4 At / In / On

When does the next train to Bilbao leave?

TICKETS

It leaves **at** twelve thirty.

Language Focus

At, **in**, and **on** are **prepositions**. Use them to talk about days, dates, times of the day, periods of time, or when things take place, e.g.,

*I was born **at** nine o'clock in the morning in December.*

Use **at** with a point of time and the word **night**.

*We're going to the movie theater **at** six o'clock.*
*My brother can't sleep **at** night.*

Use **in** with months of the year, seasons, years, and the phrases **the morning** and **the afternoon**.

*My sister's birthday is **in** summer, **in** July.*
*I was born **in** 2015.*
*What did you do **in** the afternoon?*

Use **on** with days of the week and with **morning**, **afternoon**, **evening**, and **night** when you put the day before those words.

*We have a history test **on** Wednesday.*
*What time does the bus leave **on** Saturday morning?*

---

1 Complete the sentences with *in*, *on*, or *at*.

1 Is your birthday _____**in**_____ June?

2 That movie you want to see starts _____ six o'clock.

3 We're all going to the beach _____ Saturday.

4 We went to my cousins' house _____ Sunday afternoon.

5 What time do you go to bed _____ night?

6 The train leaves at four o'clock _____ the afternoon.

2 **Correct the sentences.**

1 My birthday is on October.

   <u>My birthday is in October.</u>

2 The movie starts in seven o'clock.

   _____

3 We went swimming in the ocean on the morning.

   _____

4 My uncle and aunt came to our house for dinner at Sunday.

   _____

5 Did you see Sean at Tuesday?

   _____

6 We're going to the park in Saturday afternoon.

   _____

3 **Match 1–10 with a–j.**

1 Did your sister move to Barcelona in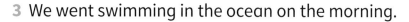

2 The dog next door to us always barks

3 What did you do

4 I'd like to go to the beach

5 Is your birthday in

6 Does the bus leave

7 I usually go to bed

8 My friends and I love to have picnics

9 My grandparents always have lunch

10 I do my homework in

a in summer. Our favorite spot is next to the river.

b on Saturday. It's going to be hot!

c 2016 or 2017?

d at 4:00, or does it leave at 4:15?

e the afternoon when I come home from school.

f November or December? Mine is in January.

g at 9:30 on weekdays. I need lots of sleep!

h at exactly one o'clock in the afternoon.

i in the morning? Did you go swimming?

j at night. Sometimes I can't sleep. It's very noisy!

Past Progressive and Simple Past

We **were playing tennis** when it **started** to rain.

Language Focus

Use **past progressive** and **simple past** together to talk about one action interrupting another in the past.

When you describe two actions using these tenses, you can order the sentence in two ways. You can put the past progressive action first followed by the **simple past**

I was doing my homework when my computer broke.

You can also put the **simple past** first followed by the **past progressive**. When you write the sentence in this way, use a comma.

When my computer broke, I was doing my homework.

1 Complete the sentences with the correct form of the verbs from the box. Use either the past progressive or simple past.

> meet   play   ~~wait~~   do   fall   begin

1 I __**was waiting**__ for the train when I saw my friend.

2 When my brother came home, I _____ my homework.

3 We were playing soccer when it _____ to snow.

4 Mom was living in Ankara when she _____ Dad.

5 My brother _____ basketball when he broke his leg.

6 My sister was doing her geography homework when she _____ asleep.

2 **Circle the correct words to complete the sentences.**

1 When I (bumped)/ *was bumping* into the tree, I was running after the soccer ball.

2 I *watched* / *was watching* TV when you called me.

3 When we *were seeing* / *saw* Ms. Gunn, the history teacher, we were waiting for a train.

4 We *were sunbathing* / *sunbathed* when it started to rain. We ran into a café nearby to stay dry!

5 My dad was walking down the street when he *was finding* / *found* the bag.

6 My brother was making a salad for lunch when he *cut* / *was cutting* his finger.

3 **Write the underlined verbs in the story in the simple past or past progressive.**

I (1) <u>am walking</u> through the park on my way home from town when I (2) <u>see</u> a large bear standing in front of me. It (3) <u>is playing</u> the violin. "Good afternoon," (4) <u>says</u> the bear. "Oh," I (5) <u>say</u>, "good afternoon." I (6) <u>am thinking</u> of starting to run when the bear (7) <u>says</u>, "I'm not a real bear, you know. This is just a special suit. I'm playing at a children's party later." The bear (8) <u>wants</u> to practice before the show. I (9) <u>listen</u> for a while. She (10) <u>isn't</u> bad, for a bear.

1 _____was walking_____ 6 _____

2 _____ 7 _____

3 _____ 8 _____

4 _____ 9 _____

5 _____ 10 _____

Reading: A Newspaper Article

1 Read the newspaper article, then answer the questions.

The Globe

March 5th

Dog Rolls Down Escalator

There was great excitement at King's Cross railway station this morning when a small dog rolled all the way down an escalator. Cuddles, a three-year-old Yorkshire terrier belonging to Mrs. Cynthia Bolton, 48, of Newcastle, wasn't hurt, but his owner was shocked.

Mrs. Bolton said, "We bought our tickets at the ticket office and then walked to the escalator. Cuddles and I were standing at the top of it

when I heard the announcer make his announcement: 'The train now arriving at Platform 4 is the 9:52 to Glasgow.' 'Quick!' I said to Cuddles. 'That's our train!' I ran forward, slipped on a bit of paper on the floor, and dropped the dog. Cuddles rolled all the way down the escalator, landing in a backpack at the bottom. Before I knew what was happening, I saw a man pick up the backpack, with Cuddles inside, and walk onto the train. 'Stop!' I shouted. 'That man has my Cuddles!'"

Other passengers were also surprised. "We were walking up the stairs," said John Maloney.

"What happened was just amazing! We put our suitcases down and stopped where we were. We wanted to see what was going on."

Mrs. Bolton didn't think twice. She ran down the escalator as fast she could, jumped onto the train, found the passenger, and managed to get her dog back. Cuddles was fine, and the pair made their journey home.

1 How old is Mrs. Bolton? __48__

2 What platform did the announcer talk about? _____

3 What was Mrs. Bolton doing when she heard the announcement? _____

_____

4 What did Mrs. Bolton slip on? _____

5 What did Cuddles fall into? _____

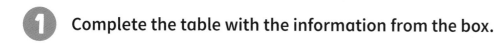
1 Complete the table with the information from the box.

> "It was terrible. They got on without paying for a ticket."
>
> "Everyone has to pay to ride the train. The rules are for everyone."
>
> Two boys got onto a train without a ticket.
>
> The transportation police asked the boys to get off the train.
>
> On Platform 3 at Liverpool Street Station in London.

What Happened	
Where It Happened	
What People Said	
What Happened in the End	

Help with Writing

Newspaper articles often include things that people said about the story. Reporters add these to make their articles more interesting for the reader.

2 Imagine you write for a newspaper. Write an article about what happened at Liverpool Street Station. Use the information in Activity 1 and the newspaper article about Cuddles to help you. Include:

- a title for the article
- the names of the two boys
- where they wanted to go
- the names of the other people in Activity 1

Listening: Tickets, Please!

1 🎧 **09** **Listen to the conversation. Answer the questions.**

1 Where does Samuel want to go?

   <u>He wants to go to Cambridge.</u>

2 How many tickets does Samuel buy?

   _____

3 What is Samuel's mom doing?

   _____

4 How much does Samuel pay for the tickets?

   _____

5 Which platform does the train leave from?

   _____

6 When does the next train leave?

   _____

2 🎧 **10** **Listen to Diana's story. Complete the sentences.**

1 Every year, Diana and her dad watch a theater play in <u>London</u>.

2 Last Saturday morning, Diana and her dad were at the _____ _____.

3 Diana's dad bought a _____ of _____ and some apple juice there.

4 When the train arrived at _____ 1, Diana's dad was feeling worried.

5 Diana's dad couldn't find the _____ for the theater.

6 When Diana and her dad got to the theater, lots of people were waiting in front of the _____ _____.

7 The man at the desk gave the _____ to Diana's dad.

8 Diana and her dad walked up the _____ to get to their seats. They loved the play.

1 Look at the departures board. Play the guessing game.

> It leaves from Platform 1.

> When does it leave?

> It leaves at eleven thirty.

> It's the train to Cardiff!

🚆 Departures

City	Platform	Time
Oxford	3	11:00
Cambridge	5	11:00
Cardiff	1	11:30
Glasgow	4	11:30
Manchester	4	12:15
London	5	12:15
Liverpool	3	01:45
Leeds	1	01:45

2 Draw a departures board with four cities from your country. Talk about your board.

> The train to Córdoba leaves from Platform 3. It leaves at two fifteen

Help with Speaking

When you buy things, don't forget to say please and thank you to the salesclerk. It is good to be polite!

3 Work with a friend. Use each other's departures boards. Buy tickets.

> Hello. Can I have a ticket to Miami, please?

> Yes, of course. One-way or round-trip?

> One-way. How much is that?

> That's twelve dollars, please.

> Here you go.

> Thanks. Here's your ticket.

> Thank you very much.

5 Used To

When you were a little baby, you used to cry all the time!

Language Focus

Use **used to** to talk about things you did routinely in the past or the way things were in the past, e.g.,

*My grandmother **used to** be a teacher. She **used to** teach Spanish.*

When we use **used to**, we are saying that things are different now:

*My sister **used to** play the piano. (She doesn't play it now.)*

*My brother **used to** draw cartoons. (He doesn't draw them now.)*

1 Complete the sentences with the verbs from the box.

> be   ~~have~~   live   play   work   make

www.thewebsite.com

The other day, I was thinking about how things change. For example, I used to
(1) _____**have**_____ blond hair when I was younger. It's dark now. My friends and I used to
(2) _____ soccer every Saturday morning, but these days we never do that. I used
to (3) _____ with my parents and brother in a small apartment downtown, but
now we live in a big house with a yard outside the city. Dad used to (4) _____
for a newspaper, but now he works for a website. Mom used to (5) _____ a
children's television show called *Milkshake*, but now she writes stories. Grandpa used to
(6) _____ a police officer, but now he is retired. Nothing stays the same. It can be
sad sometimes, but it keeps things interesting!

44

2 Are the sentences correct or incorrect? Correct the sentences you think are incorrect.

1 David use to carry a walkie-talkie.

  <u>Incorrect.</u>   <u>David used to carry a walkie-talkie.</u>

2 Tina used to interview suspects.

  _____ _____

3 Brian used to work at a police station.

  _____ _____

4 Jerry used to wearing a uniform.

  _____ _____

5 Chris using to catch criminals.

  _____ _____

6 Jonathan used drive a fast car.

  _____ _____

3 Write sentences with *used to*. Then write what the person does or has now.

1 Ceren <u>used to play basketball.</u>
  <u>Now she plays tennis.</u>

2 Sandro _____
  _____

3 Elena _____
  _____

4 Sam _____
  _____

Had To

I'm so tired! I **had to** study all day for my big English test tomorrow.

Language Focus

Use **had to** to talk about something that someone told you to do, e.g., *Dad **had to** paint the fence this weekend. Mom told him it was looking a little dirty.*

1 Rewrite the sentences with the words in the correct order.

1 rooms / clean / we/ to / had / our   We had to clean our rooms.

2 had / homework / to / his / Dom / do

3 to / do / dishes / had / the / Marlene

4 had / clean / to / the / Sofia / windows

5 Neil / sweep / floor / had / the / to

6 walk / dog / had / Ada / to / the

7 cook / had/ Pablo / to / last / dinner / night

8 early / bed / had / Zehra / to / to / go

2 **Circle the correct verb forms to complete the text.**

My brother went to a police academy last year. Things weren't easy there! Lessons used to **(1)** (start) / *starting* at 6:00. They had to **(2)** *wore* / *wear* a uniform. They had to **(3)** *go* / *goes* running every day. They had to **(4)** *spent* / *spend* two hours every evening doing homework. They had to **(5)** *did* / *do* tests about how to be a police officer every Monday morning. Oh, and they had to **(6)** *attend* / *attending* lessons on Saturday mornings, too! He enjoyed it, but he's happy he doesn't have to go there now.

3 **Look at the pictures. Then write sentences using *had to* and the verbs from the box.**

> cook dinner ~~go grocery shopping~~
> study for a test
> take   do the dishes   clean the bathroom

1 Mick _____**had to go grocery shopping**_____
   for his grandma.

2 Marco _____
   for his family.

3 Mia _____
   on the weekend.

4 Pedro _____
   after dinner.

5 Stephanie _____
   before she could watch TV.

6 Katya _____
   her little sister to school.

Reading: A Description

1 Read the blog post, then complete the sentences.

Lou's Blog About School

March 9th

Describing Detectives

We had a really interesting class this morning. We talked about detectives. Detectives are a special type of police officer. Their job is to investigate serious crimes like murder. "My sister used to be a detective," said Mr. Garcia. "Wow!" I said. "Did she enjoy the job?" "Yes, she did," said Mr. Garcia, "but it wasn't easy." Then he told us all about his sister's job. She used to work at night and used to work long hours. She had to look for clues. She had to interview suspects. She had to work really hard to solve the crimes.

Later, Mr. Garcia asked us to describe a detective. But he didn't want us to describe a real detective. We had to invent one. We had to give our detective a name and describe his or her daily life. I called my detective Inspector Bach. This was my description of him: Inspector Bach didn't have any hair, but he had a beard and mustache. There was a scar on the end of his nose. He liked to touch the scar. Inspector Bach used to work on solving murders. He used to solve his crimes in an unusual way: by listening to music. "I always get my best ideas then," he said. Inspector Bach used to work on his own. "I like to be quiet," he said. "It helps me think."

😀 😐 ☹️
(10 comments)

1 Mr. Garcia's sister used to be a ____**detective**____.

2 Mr. Garcia's sister _____ for clues.

3 Mr. Garcia asked Lou's class to invent their own _____.

4 Lou called his detective _____.

5 Lou's detective _____ his crimes by listening to music.

1 Describe members of your family. Use the words from the box.

> beard   mustache   blond   light   dark   curly   straight   long   short

1 _____

2 _____

3 _____

4 _____

5 _____

Help with Writing

When you write a description of someone, you want the reader to imagine what they look like. You can do that by using interesting details. For example, Lou tells us that Inspector Bach had a scar on the end of his nose.

2 Invent your own detective. Write a description of him or her. Use Lou's description of Inspector Bach to help you. Include:

- your detective's name
- a description of his or her hair, eyes, height, etc.
- the things your detective used to do and had to do

My Detective   January 6th

Listening: Officers and Criminals

1 🎧 11 **Listen and write *t* (true) or *f* (false).**

1 Kelly and her mom had to buy a present for Kelly's dad. `t`

2 Kelly's dad used to be a journalist, but he isn't one now. ☐

3 Kelly was with her mom in a new pen store called *Write Now*. ☐

4 There was a clothing store where the pen store is now. ☐

5 A woman was stealing some notebooks in the pen store. ☐

6 The woman was blond, and there was a scar on her cheek. ☐

7 Kelly's mom called the police. ☐

8 The police couldn't catch the woman. ☐

2 🎧 12 **Listen to Max talk about his aunt. Put the sentences in order.**

☐ Max's aunt worked as a police officer for ten years.

`1` Max's Aunt Vicky was a police officer before she was a photographer.

☐ She had to be careful, and she used to work all night.

☐ Auntie Vicky doesn't have straight dark hair now.

☐ She had to wear a uniform, and she used to carry a walkie-talkie.

☐ Max's aunt chased and caught criminals.

1 Work with a friend. Read the news report. Then choose your questions and ask and answer.

www.dailynews.nex   Search   GO!

Robbery at Bank

There was a robbery at the North Bank. It was on Saturday afternoon at 3 p.m. The robber stole thousands of dollars and some important documents. The police are looking for a young man. He is about 30 years old. He has short, dark hair, a beard, and a mustache. The man has blue eyes, and there is a scar above his right eye. Please call the Central Police Station with any information.

BANK

Student A

Where and when was the robbery?

How old is the robber?

What does the robber have above one of his eyes?

Student B

What did the robber steal?

Can you describe the robber?

Who should you give any information to?

2 With your friend, look at the suspects for the bank robbery. Can you describe them?

> Can you describe George Nash?

> He has short, dark hair …

a

George Nash

b

Liam Walton

c

Jordan Thomas

3 Talk to your friend. Which of the suspects robbed the bank? Why do you think so?

> I think … robbed the bank because he …

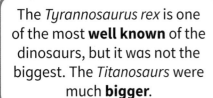

6 Comparatives and Superlatives

The *Tyrannosaurus rex* is one of the most **well known** of the dinosaurs, but it was not the biggest. The *Titanosaurs* were much **bigger**.

Tyrannosaurus rex

Language Focus

Use **comparatives** to compare two people, places, or things, e.g., *Josep is faster than Marco*.

Add **-er** to adjectives with one syllable, e.g., **slower**.

Remove **-y** and add **-ier** to adjectives with two syllables ending in **-y**, e.g., **happier**.

Put **more** before most adjectives of two or more syllables, e.g., **more difficult**.

Use **superlatives** to say one thing or person in a group has the most of a particular quality, e.g., *Josep is **the fastest runner** I know*.

Add **-est** to adjectives with one syllable, e.g., **the slowest**.

Remove **-y** and add **-iest** to adjectives with two syllables ending in **-y**, e.g., **the happiest**.

Put **the most** before most adjectives of two or more syllables, e.g., **the most difficult**.

There are some **irregular forms**, e.g., **better / the best**, **worse / the worst**.

---

1 Write the comparatives and the superlatives.

1 big   _____bigger_____   _____the biggest_____

2 strong   _____   _____

3 heavy   _____   _____

4 friendly   _____   _____

5 dangerous   _____   _____

6 beautiful   _____   _____

2 Rewrite the sentences with the words in the correct order.

1 lions / are / smaller / domestic / than / much / cats / .

Domestic cats are much smaller than lions.

2 in / biggest / world / some / the / are / animals / elephants / the / of / .

_____

3 interesting / beasts / are / than / real / more / mythical / animals / .

_____

4 are / dangerous/ the / Africa / mosquitos / animals / in / most / ?

_____

5 fastest / cheetah / animal / the / the / land / is / .

_____

6 necks / kangaroos / than / giraffes / longer / have / .

_____

3 Complete the text with the comparative or superlative form of the adjectives.

My parents gave me a great present for my birthday: *The Dictionary of Mythical Beasts*. It is the **(1)** <u>most interesting</u> (interesting) book I know. It taught me about unicorns, Pegasus, and the sphinx. I read it every morning before breakfast and every night before I fall asleep. One evening, after dinner, I couldn't find it anywhere. "Oh, no!" I said. "This is **(2)** _____ (bad) day of my life! Where is my book, Fred? Help me!" But my brother was too busy playing *The Phoenix Rises*, his new video game. "It's much **(3)** _____ (exciting) than your old book," he said. "No, it's not," I said. "My book teaches me things. Your game is just for fun." "But when I play it," said Fred, "I learn how to see things that move quickly. I see them **(4)** _____ (good) than I did before. This morning, for example, I saw Roger running really fast into the yard." Roger is our dog. "He had something in his mouth. It looked **(5)** _____ (heavy) than his toy bones. I took it from him before up he could chew on it. Take a look over there." I found my book in Roger's basket. On its cover were marks from Roger's teeth, but it was OK. "Thanks, Fred," I said. "You're **(6)** _____ (good) brother in the world! Can you show me how to play *The Phoenix Rises*?"

It Looks Like ...

It looks like a really big ape!

Language Focus

Use **it looks like** to talk about the appearance of someone or something, e.g., *Unicorns* **look like** *horses*.

The phrase is used to ask about someone's or something's appearance.

*What does your brother **look like**? He's tall and has short, black hair.*

Note that **looks like** is not used in the reply.

It's also used to compare appearances.

*Who does your sister **look like**? She **looks like** my mom.*

*Look at that cloud! It **looks like** a face.*

1 Correct the sentences.

1 Who are your brother look like?

   Who does your brother look like?

2 Who do you looking like?

   _____

3 Does a centaur looks like a man?

   _____

4 What do mermaids look liking?

   _____

2 **Match the answers with the questions in Activity 1.**

a Well, I have short, black hair and brown eyes. I look like my dad. ☐

b He looks a little bit like my mom. They both have long noses. 1

c Yes and no. They have the head and body of a man but the legs of a horse. ☐

d They look like women, but with fish tails instead of legs. ☐

3 **Complete the description with the words from the box.**

like   it   looks   does   ~~look~~

The Dictionary of
Mythical
Beasts

L Is for the Loch Ness Monster

What do mythical creatures **(1)** _____**look**_____ like? Well, they are all different. It depends on the imagination of their creators. The Loch Ness Monster is the most famous mythical beast of the United Kingdom. People come from all over the world, hoping to see this creature swimming around in a large lake in the Highlands of Scotland.

What **(2)** _____ it look like? Nobody knows, of course, but some people who believe it exists say that it **(3)** _____ like a dinosaur, while others say **(4)** _____ looks like a dragon. It has a long neck and a small head. Take a look at the picture. What do you think it looks **(5)** _____?

1 Read about the babirusa, then complete descriptions a–e with words from the box.

The **Babirusa**

The babirusa is not the most famous animal in the world, but it is certainly one of the most interesting. The word "babirusa" itself is Malay and means "pig-deer," although the animals look more like pigs than deer. These wild pigs live in the forests of Indonesia and are endangered. There are fewer than 10,000 of them left.

There are four species of babirusa. The most well-known of the species are brown or gray in color and have tails up to 32 centimeters in length. They eat fruit, grasses, and leaves, as well as other small animals. The males are larger than the females. Like elephants and walruses, these animals have large teeth that come out of their mouths. But babirusas are unusual. The upper tusks of the males come out of their snouts, not their mouths. They look like horns.

deer   ~~tusks~~   walrus   forest   snout

a A set of large pointed teeth, like those of an elephant. _____**tusks**_____

b An animal that moves fast. The males have horns called antlers. _____

c A large area of land covered with trees. _____

d The nose of an animal, especially that of a pig. _____

e An animal that lives in and around the ocean at the North Pole. It has thick skin and two long tusks. _____

1 Complete the table with the information from the box.

The rainforests of Madagascar   Aye-aye

Is nocturnal, so sleeps in the day

Insects and fruit   Spends its life in trees

Has big eyes and ears and a tail longer than its body

Doesn't look like a primate but is related to apes, chimps, and humans

Name	
Where It Lives	
What It Looks Like	
How It Lives	
What It Eats	

2 Write about the aye-aye. Use the information in the table in Activity 1 and the description of the babirusa to help you.

Help with Writing

A short description of an animal should give as much information as possible in a few words. Try to answer possible questions in your description, e.g., *How big is it? How long does it live?*

Listening: The Terrible Omnix

1 🎧 13 **Listen and number the pictures in the correct order.**

a

b ☐

c 1

d ☐

e ☐

f ☐

2 🎧 14 **Listen to the conversation. Circle the correct words.**

1 (Edward)/ *Laura* is reading *The Terrible Omnix*.

2 The Trussock and the *Munkle* / *Arkle* look like crocodiles.

3 The smallest beast in the forest looks like a *monkey* / *dragon*.

4 The Galloping Runnyback is *Edward's* / *Laura's* favorite beast.

5 The Ginocat is *more beautiful* / *uglier* that the Galloping Runnyback.

6 The Gagger is *faster* / *slower* than the Ginocat.

7 The Gagger looks like a *stegosaurus* / *T-Rex*.

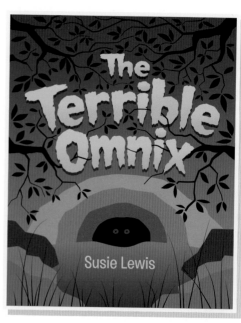

The Terrible Omnix

Susie Lewis

1 Look at the advertisement. Write answers. Then practice.

A New Beast for Maya's Forest!

The author of *The Terrible Omnix*, Susie Lewis, is looking for a new beast for Maya's adventures. Can you think of one? Answer the questions and send your ideas to theterribleomnix@fantasybooks.com. Good luck!

1 What's your beast's name?

_____

2 Where in the forest does the beast live?

_____

3 What does the beast look like?

_____

4 What can it do?

_____

5 Who are the beast's friends?

_____

2 Work with a friend. Talk about your beast. Ask and answer the questions in Activity 1.

> What's your beast's name?

> It's called the Birdix.

> It's called the Giant Flapalot. What's your beast's name?

3 Work with another friend. Tell them about your friend's beast from Activity 2.

> Luke's beast is called the Birdix. It lives in the biggest tree in the forest. It looks like a bird, but it has four wings. It can fly very fast. Its friends are the Munkle and the Ginocat.

7 Possessive Pronouns

That's not **ours**. It's **theirs**.

Language Focus

Use **possessive pronouns** to talk about things that belong to you, e.g., *Is this Jon's case? No, it's* **mine**.

Possessive Adjective		Possessive Pronoun	
my	your	mine	yours
his	her	his	hers
our	their	ours	theirs

1 Circle the correct words to complete the sentences.

1 Is this Leo's coat?

Yes, it's *hers /* (*his*).

2 Look! These are *his / our* scooters!

Yes! That's mine, and that's yours, Antonio!

3 Is that her violin?

No, it's not. *Hers / Mine* is over there.

4 These aren't my pencils. Are they *yours / hers?*

No, they aren't mine.

5 Are you sure this violin is Tom and Deb's?

Yes, it's *theirs / ours.* I saw them with it earlier.

6 Is that the guitar you parents got you for your birthday?

No, it isn't. *Mine / Yours* is at home.

2 Rewrite the sentences with possessive pronouns.

1 It's my tractor.   It's mine.

2 Is that your car?   _____

3 That's his book.   _____

4 It's her keyboard.   _____

5 These are our instruments. _____

6 Are these their bags?   _____

3 Replace the underlined words with possessive pronouns.

It was my saxophone, not Toni's. "This is (1) my saxophone," Toni said. "It's not (2) her saxophone," I said to my friend. "It's (3) my saxophone." Toni had her own saxophone. "That's (4) your saxophone," I said. "But I don't like that one," she said. That happened all the time. Toni always wanted what other people had. "Harry brought his keyboard to school today," she told me once. "He wanted to practice at lunchtime. I told him it wasn't (5) his keyboard." "Whose did you say it was?" I asked, knowing what the answer was going to be. (6) "My keyboard!"

One morning, at breakfast, I decided to let Toni know what she was like. She sat down at the table with some toast. "Thanks for the toast," I said. "It's not (7) your toast," she said. "Yes, it is," I said. "It's (8) my toast." I did that every day for a week. She wasn't very happy with me, but I didn't stop saying that all the toast she made was (9) my toast. "OK, OK," she said a week later. "It's (10) your toast and my toast."

1 _____mine_____   6 _____

2 _____   7 _____

3 _____   8 _____

4 _____   9 _____

5 _____   10 _____

Who / That / Where

This is the house **where** Callum lives.

Language Focus

Who, **that**, and **where** are **relative pronouns**. Use these words to give more information about a person, thing, or place.

*Anya's the girl **who** lives in my street.*

*The book **that** I got for my birthday is called* How To Play The Guitar.

*The town **where** Omer lives has a great new movie theater.*

1 Circle the correct relative pronouns to complete the sentences.

1 The theater _____ we played our first concert is the oldest in our town.

  a who   b that   c (where)

2 The cookies _____ my brother and sister made are delicious.

  a who   b that   c where

3 The girl _____ joined our class last week is from Bodrum.

  a who   b that   c where

4 The video game _____ I bought this weekend is great.

  a who   b that   c where

5 The town _____ my grandparents live is high in the mountains.

  a who   b that   c where

6 The boy _____ lives next door to us plays the harp really well.

  a who   b that   c where

2 Check ✓ the correct sentences.

1 a Yesterday I bought a keyboard that is from the U.S. ✓
  b Yesterday I bought a keyboard who is from the U.S. ☐

2 a Look, there's the girl where lives next door to my grandparents! ☐
  b Look, there's the girl who lives next door to my grandparents! ☐

3 a The car that my brother drives is black. ☐
  b The car who my brother drives is black. ☐

4 a Martina is the girl who comes from Mexico. ☐
  b Martina is the girl where comes from Mexico. ☐

5 a The park that we play tennis is near my house. ☐
  b The park where we play tennis is near my house. ☐

6 a The instrument who Furkan plays is the piano. ☐
  b The instrument that Furkan plays is the piano. ☐

3 Complete the information about the festival with *who*, *that*, or *where*.

Summer Fest

Summer Fest is for people **(1)** _____who_____ love all types of music. It's the festival **(2)** _____ everyone enjoys!

We have jazz, pop, rock, classical, and hip-hop. Oh, and folk too! And we have the perfect location. Hendrix Hall is the place **(3)** _____ the festival happens. It has a lake, tree-lined walks, and lots of picnic spots.

Tickets cost $60. For people **(4)** _____ are under 16, we even have a special price: $45!

Mat and Jen are the people **(5)** _____ organize the festival. They know everything! If you want to ask them a question, email them at matandjen@summerfestival.com. But the only thing **(6)** _____ you really need to know is this: be ready to dance! See you there.

1 Read the advertisement, then complete the sentences.

1 Des Paul created the guitar in _____1956_____.

2 Many famous _____ play the Des Paul Fretocaster.

3 It usually costs _____.

4 You can buy it for a special price: _____.

5 The special price is available for only _____.

6 You can buy the guitar online or in _____.

1 Add more instruments to the instrument word families below.

String Family	guitar,
Percussion Family	
Wind Family	

Help with Writing

Advertisements try to make readers feel something. When we are excited or happy, advertisers think we are more likely to want to spend money. Look at the advertisement for the guitar. The Des Paul is "beautiful," and it's "the instrument of guitar heroes." The advertisement uses these phrases to make people want to own one of the guitars.

2 Write an advertisement for a musical instrument. Use the advertisement for the Fretocaster to help you write yours. Include:

- the name of the instrument
- the people who play it
- the places where you can buy it
- the types of music that you can play with it
- the price

Listening: Music

1 🎧 **15** **Listen and check ☑ the correct picture.**

1 Which guitar is Henry's?

a ☐ b ☐ c ☑

2 Which tambourine does Kate play?

a ☐ b ☐ c ☐

3 Which instrument is Lily going to play?

a ☐ b ☐ c ☐

4 Which keyboard is Tony's?

a ☐ b ☐ c ☐

5 Which instrument does Ruby play?

a ☐ b ☐ c ☐

2 🎧 **16** **Listen and match.**

a b c d e

1 Oliver   **2** Ava   **3** Ivy   **4** Amelia   **5** Lucas

1 Look and write. Then play the description game. Use the words in the boxes.

> The instrument that I play is small. You hit it or shake it.

> You play a percussion instrument: the tambourine!

> blow into   hit   shake   pluck

> string   percussion   wind

1
harp

2
_____

3
_____

4
_____

5
_____

6
_____

2 Draw a special musical instrument. Complete and practice.

This is called a _____.
It's a (string / percussion / wind)
_____ instrument.
It's (big / small) _____ and it
looks like _____.
To play it, you have to _____.

Help with Speaking

When you describe an object, say the object's name. Then you can talk about its size, shape, and color. You can also tell people how it works and how to use it.

3 Talk about your musical instrument.

> This is called a key guitar. It's a string and a percussion instrument. It's big and it looks like a box. To play it, you have to pluck the strings and hit the keys.

8 Will

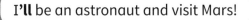

I'll be an astronaut and visit Mars!

What will you be when you grow up?

Language Focus

Use **will** to make predictions about the future, e.g., *I think Patrick **will** be a soccer player.*

Yes/No question form:

***Will** we live on the moon one day?*
*Yes, we **will**. / No, we won't.*

"Wh" question form:

***What will** the weather be like next week?*   *I think it **will** be hot and sunny.*

The contracted form of **will** is **'ll**, e.g., **I'll**, **she'll**, **we'll**.

Both **will** and **going to** can be used to make predictions. We usually use **going to** when we are more certain that something is going to happen. For example, looking up at a black cloud in the sky, we say, "It's going to rain," not ~~"It will rain"~~.

---

1 **Complete the sentences with the verbs from the box.**

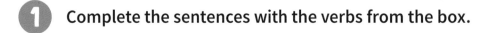

have   travel   be   live   ~~catch~~   work

1 Will you _____**catch**_____ dangerous criminals when you're a police officer, Jess?

2 When I grow up, I'll _____ in a hospital.

3 Will we all _____ on the moon one day?

4 I think it will _____ hot this weekend.

5 When I grow up, my friends and I will _____ around the world.

6 We'll _____ lots of fun at Elliot's birthday party.

2 **Rewrite the sentences with the words in the correct order.**

1 be / what / you / will   What will you be _____ ?

2 you / will / where / work   _____ ?

3 will / live / another country / in / you   _____ ?

4 you / of house / will / what type / in / live   _____ ?

5 meet / you / who / will   _____ ?

6 where / will / travel / you   _____ ?

7 learn / will / you / what / languages   _____ ?

8 will / you / what / do / your / free time / in   _____ ?

3 **Answer the questions in Activity 2 so they are true for you.**

My Future Blog

My Future

I was thinking about my future the other day. These are my predictions for my life …

1 _____

2 _____

3 _____

4 _____

5 _____

6 _____

7 _____

8 _____

Adverbs

It was the last day of school before summer vacation. The children walked home, singing songs **loudly** in the afternoon sun.

Language Focus

Use **adverbs** to say how someone does, did, or will do an action, e.g., *The ambulance driver drove **quickly***.

We form many adverbs by adding **-ly** to an adjective:

quick – quick**ly**   bad – bad**ly**   loud – loud**ly**

If an adjective ends in **y**, we change the **y** to an **i** and add **-ly**:

angry – angr**ily**   happy – happ**ily**   heavy – heav**ily**

Some adverbs have an irregular form:

good – well   hard – hard   fast – fast

1   **Write the adverbs.**

1 quick _____**quickly**_____   4 careful _____

2 dangerous _____   5 bad _____

3 beautiful _____   6 heavy _____

2 Complete the email with the adverb form of the words from the box.

good ~~quiet~~ loud happy slow quick

To siobhan.odonnell@redworld.com **From** liam.kerr@zmail.com

Subject Our Trip to the Planetarium

Hi, Aunt Siobhan,

The other night, my friends and I went with our parents to a special "Evening with the Stars" event at the planetarium in town. We met Neil Collins. He used to be an astronaut! He gave us a tour, but he spoke so **(1)** _____quietly_____ that we couldn't hear him very **(2)** _____. We wanted to say, "Please could you speak more **(3)** _____, Mr. Collins?" but we were all very nervous because he was a famous astronaut.

We saw lots of very interesting things. My favorite was a huge telescope. Mr. Collins let us move it around. We looked at one part of the night sky, then another. It was very heavy, so we could only move it really **(4)** _____. It needed two of us to move it! We were about to go when Mr. Collins called us back. "Come **(5)** _____, everyone. Look, you can see Venus! It's so clear we don't even need the telescope!" We all looked up **(6)** _____, so excited to be with this famous astronaut who was telling us all about the planets. When I got home, I downloaded his special space app!

Love, Liam

3 Complete the sentences with adverbs.

1 My grandpa drove so _____slowly_____ that it took us a long time to get home.

2 My brother ran _____ and won the race.

3 I walked _____ downstairs because I didn't want anyone to hear me.

4 Hold that vase _____, Tom! You don't want to drop it.

5 My sister did _____ on her English exam. She got 89%!

6 I played _____ and lost the tennis match 6–2, 6–1.

Reading: A Diary Entry

1 Read Jana's diary and write *t* (true) or *f* (false). Correct the false sentences.

Wednesday, March 16th

"Please come," said Emre. "It will be amazing!"

"But I don't like movies about space," I said.

"Everyone is going. Come on, Jana. We'll have a good time."

I really didn't want to go the movie theater this afternoon. All my friends get so excited about movies with special effects, but I find them really boring. You know, astronauts on space stations, rockets whizzing through the sky, explosions, UFOs. It's not for me. I said to Emre, "It will be really boring."

"Well," he said slowly, "maybe it will be boring, but there is only one way to find out."

The movie is called *The Comet*. It's about an astronaut who has to fix her space station,

then ride a comet across space to save Earth. Really, really silly. But I loved it! Emre laughed at me after the movie because I was talking so much and so quickly. "And that part with the two moons, and the scene when the astronaut went up in the rocket through the stars, and, and ...!"

"You see?" said Emre. "I knew you would have a good time!"

1 Emre didn't want Jana to go to the movie theater.

   [f]   He asked her to go to the movie theater.

2 Jana didn't want to go to the movie theater.

   ☐ _____

3 Jana likes movies about space.

   ☐ _____

4 Jana thought the idea for the movies was very interesting.

   ☐ _____

5 Jana liked the movie.

   ☐ _____

1 Complete the sentences from the diary with the words from the box.

> everyone   great   be   'll   ~~come~~

1 Please ____**come**____ .

2 It will be _____ .

3 _____ is going.

4 We _____ have a good time.

5 It will _____ really boring.

Help with Writing

People often write diaries to record not only their feelings but also the most interesting things that they do. That means that in the future, they can look back at the past and remember some of their favorite times.

2 Write a diary entry for one day last week. Try to use *will* and adverbs. Choose one of the following two events to write about:

- You went to the movie theater with your friends. You watched a movie about an astronaut. You wanted to go, but you didn't like the movie.
- You went to the planetarium with your family. You learned about the planets. You didn't want to go, but you had a good time.

_____   _____
_____   _____
_____   _____
_____   _____
_____   _____
_____   _____
_____   _____
_____   _____

Listening: Astronauts

1 🎧 17 Listen to the astronaut's story.
Complete the sentences.

1 Robert was on the Moon X27 ____ **mission** ____ .

2 Rachel is the newest _____ on Robert's team.

3 The team's _____ wasn't working, and they couldn't fix it.

4 The team couldn't talk to the astronauts on the _____ _____ .

5 Robert listened _____ to Rachel's idea.

6 Rachel's idea worked and the team came back home _____ .

2 🎧 18 Listen to the interview. Answer the questions.

1 Why is Rachel famous now?

  Because she helped to fix the Moon X27 rocket. _____

2 What will Rachel and her team do next?

  _____

3 What does Rachel say about space missions?

  _____

4 Where will Rachel go on her next mission?

  _____

5 When will her next mission be?

  _____

6 Who will go with Rachel on the mission?

  _____

  _____

1 **Read the predictions. Talk about them with a friend.**

In the future …

1 people will go on vacation to the moon.

2 we will travel on rockets.

3 there will be a telescope in every home.

4 some people will live on Mars.

5 astronauts will find life on another planet.

> Will people go on vacation to the moon? What do you think?

> I don't think they will. But I think we'll travel on rockets.

2 **With your friend, imagine you are astronauts. What do you need for your space mission? Use the ideas in the box and your ideas.**

> We need a telescope.

> Why?

a telescope   walkie-talkies   a soccer ball
spacesuits   computer games

> It will help us to look at stars and comets. What about walkie-talkies?

3 **With your friend, plan your space mission. Where would you like to go? Decide on three places.**

> Let's go to the moon first.

> Great idea! What about the International Space Station next?

4 **Talk about your space mission.**

> Paula and I will go to the moon first. Next, we'll …

9 A Bottle / Can / Loaf / Bag / Piece Of ...

OK, for our picnic, we need two **loaves of** bread, a **bottle of** water, and a big **piece of** cheese!

Language Focus

Use **a bottle** / **can** / **loaf** / **bag** / **piece of** to talk about the quantity of something or what something is contained in.

Use **bottle of** with water, orange juice, lemonade, milk.

Use **can of** with lemonade, tomatoes, pears, peas.

Use **loaf of** with bread. The plural of **loaf** is **loaves**.

Use **bag of** with cookies, chips.

Use **piece of** with cheese, cake.

1 Correct the sentences.

1 Can we get a loaf of cookies, please?

Can we get a bag of cookies, please?

2 I'm going to buy a bottle of tomatoes from the store.

_____

3 Who would like this last can of cheese?

_____

4 We need a bottle of chips and some chocolate.

_____

5 I'd like two cans of bread, please.

_____

6 There was a new piece of milk in the fridge yesterday.

_____

2 Complete the dialogue with the words from the box.

> piece bottles bags bottle ~~loaf~~ pieces bag loaves

Marie   We have one (1) _____loaf_____ of bread. Is that enough?

Carl   No, we need two (2) _____ for the four of us.

Marie   OK. What about something to drink?

Carl   Well, Stefan has two (3) _____ of water, and I have
a (4) _____ of orange juice.

Marie   Do we need anything else? A (5) _____ of cookies, maybe?

Carl   No, Jeremy has that. You know his sweet tooth. He's going to bring two
(6) _____ of cookies and a big (7) _____ of cake
for everyone.

Marie   Really? I think that's everything, then. Oh, cheese?

Carl   I have that. I cut three big (8) _____ this morning and
put them in my bag.

Marie   Great!

3 Use the notes below, and words for containers, to write a shopping list.

~~2 × bread~~   1 × cookies   6 × chips

3 × milk   2 × tomatoes   1 × corn

2 × water   1 × pears

Shopping List

1 Two loaves of bread _____

2 _____

3 _____

4 _____

5 _____

6 _____

7 _____

8 _____

How Much / How Many?

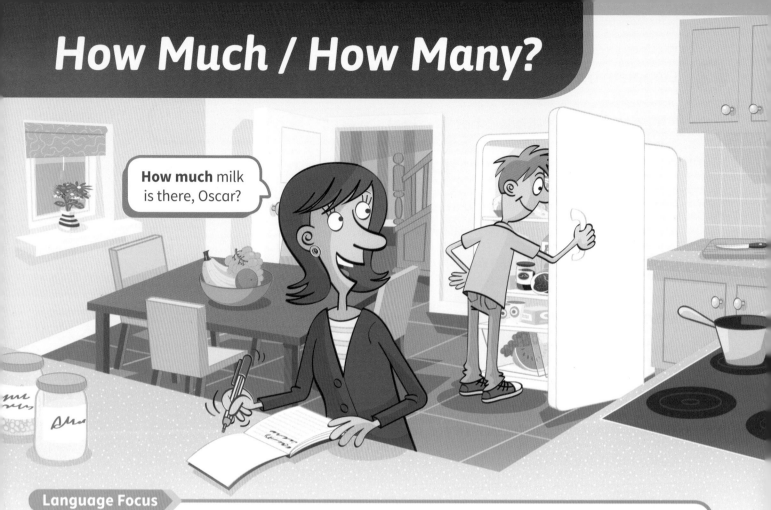

How much milk is there, Oscar?

Language Focus

Use **How much / How many?** to ask about the quantity of something, e.g., **How much** cheese do we need?

Use **how much** with uncountable nouns such as cheese, milk, water, rice.

Use **how many** with countable nouns such as carrots, loaves, bags, pieces.

Note that when we use **how many** with an uncountable noun, we make only the container plural, e.g., How many bottles of water? not ~~How many bottles of waters?~~

1 **Circle the correct words to complete the sentences.**

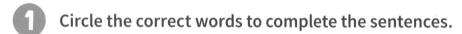

1 How *many* / *much* eggs do you need for the omelette?

2 How *many* / *much* bars of chocolate are there in the cabinet?

3 How *many* / *much* pieces of cheese would you like?

4 How *many* / *much* bottles of milk are there in the fridge?

5 How *many* / *much* bread do you want?

6 How *many* / *much* water do you think we need?

2 Match the questions in Activity 1 with the answers below.

a I can see only one. Mom finished the other bottle this morning. ☐ 4

b Get me two small loaves, please. ☐

c One big piece. ☐

d I think six will be enough. ☐

e Quite a lot. It's going to be a hot day. ☐

f There aren't any. I think Dad ate them all! ☐

3 Complete the questions about the picture with *much* or *many*. Then answer them with *There is* / *There are*.

1 How __many__ cans of tomatoes are there?   There are two cans of tomatoes.

2 How _____ bags of chips are there?   _____

3 How _____ bread is there?   _____

4 How _____ chocolate is there?   _____

5 How _____ apples are there?   _____

6 How _____ cans of carrots are there?   _____

Reading: A Letter

1 Read the letter, then order the information in sentences a–g.

Dear Students,

As you know, next Friday is the camping trip to the Northern Mountains for three days of hiking and cooking outdoors. We're all looking forward to it.

I am writing to you in order to give you some important information about the trip. We will set out from the school parking lot at six o'clock on Friday morning, so please make sure you are at the gates by at least 5:45. That is a very early start, I know. Set your alarms!

It will take two hours to drive to the Northern Mountains. Please bring some music to listen to, a book to read, or a game of some type to play with your friends. You should also bring a bottle of water and something to eat, maybe a sandwich, a piece of fruit, and a bag of chips.

As soon as we get to the campsite, we will put up our tents. The teachers are ready to help students with that. After that, we plan to spend the afternoon outside. There are ropes to swing on and a lake to dive into and swim in. Remember to bring your swimsuits! We are going to organize boat trips throughout the weekend. Students can take turns sailing the small boats.

All students will have special duties over the weekend. Some will make breakfast, others will collect wood. One group will make a big raft. The teachers will tell you on the first day who is in which group.

One final thing, the question students usually ask before the trip is, "How many people will sleep in each tent?" I can answer that question now. The tents are very big, and four students will sleep in each one.

If you would like further information about the trip, do not hesitate to call me in my office between 10 a.m. and 2 p.m., Monday to Friday.

Sincerely yours,

Elanur Berker

a how long the trip is ☐

b where the students are going ☐

c how many students in a tent ☐

d things students need to bring ☐

e when to call the office ☐

f things students will do in the Northern Mountains ☐

g when the trip starts [1]

1 **Answer the questions about your country.**

1 Where are the best places to go camping? _____

2 What can you do in those places? _____

3 When will the weather be the best in those places? _____

Help with Writing

When we write formal letters, we begin them with *Dear ...,*
When a writer wants to be very formal, he or she can
finish the letter with *Sincerely yours,*.

2 **Imagine you are the principal of a school. You are going to write a letter telling students about a camping trip in your country. Plan the letter by making notes. Include:**

- when it is
- where it is
- how long the trip is
- things students need to bring on the trip
- activities students will do on the trip

3 **Now write your letter. Use the letter on the Reading page and your notes from Activity 2 to help you.**

_____

_____

_____

_____

_____

_____

_____

_____

_____

Listening: A Camping Trip

1 🎧 19 **What does Jake want to do at the campsite? Listen and check ☑ or put an X ☒.**

At the campsite, Jake wants to ...

dive into the lake	☑
make a fire	☐
collect wood	☐
sail a boat	☐
make a raft	☐
swing on a rope	☐
wash and dry clothes	☐
put up the tent	☐

2 🎧 20 **Listen to Suzie and her dad. Circle the correct answers.**

1 How much water do they have?

  a Four bottles.   (b) Five bottles.

2 How much bread do they have?

  a Two loaves.   b Three loaves.

3 How many cans of soup are there?

  a Five.   b Six.

4 Is there any rice in the box?

  a Yes, there's one bag.   b No, there isn't any.

5 What fruit does Suzie want?

  a Bananas.   b Apples.

6 How much chocolate do they take?

  a Two small bars.   b Two big bars.

1 Imagine you are going on a camping trip. What would you like to take? Draw four things and say.

> I'd like to take my book, a bar of chocolate, …

2 Look and check ☑ six things you need for your camping trip. Then ask a friend and check ☑ the things they need.

> Do you need any pasta?

> Yes, I do. What about you?

> I don't. But I need some bread.

Food and Drinks	Me	My Friend
pasta		
bread		
water		
milk		
apples		
soup		
tomatoes		
eggs		

3 With your friend, look at your table in Activity 2. Ask and answer questions with *How much* and *How many*.

> How much pasta do you need?

> I need four loaves.

> I need two bags. How much bread do you need?

Audioscripts

Welcome Unit page 10

 01

Daisy Mike, do you like going on adventures?

Mike Yes, of course, Daisy! Adventures are exciting!

Daisy So, what do you like doing?

Mike Well, I like hiking in the mountains. I always discover amazing places and animals in the mountains.

Daisy Wow! Who do you go with?

Mike I go with my cousins, every summer. They live near the mountains. You can come next summer!

Daisy Hmm, thanks, but I don't really like the mountains … I prefer the city. I like riding the big roller coaster at the amusement park!

Mike The big roller coaster? Really? I hate going on that one. I'm scared of it! But I love driving the bumper cars. What about you?

Daisy Me too! The bumper cars are fun!

Mike And I also like looking for treasure. My brother and I are good at finding treasure in different places.

Daisy Hmm … I don't like doing that. I never find any treasure! But I like exploring caves. What about you, Mike?

Mike Of course! I love exploring caves. Last weekend, I found some bats in one!

Daisy What an adventure! Let's plan an exploring trip!

Mike Yes! What about next weekend?

Daisy Great idea!

 02

Jess Hi, Jacob. How was your climbing trip?

Jacob It was amazing, Jess!

Jess Did you go to Castle Mountain?

Jacob No, we didn't. We went to Cave Mountain.

Jess Wow! Cave Mountain is far. How did you get there? Did you go by train?

Jacob No, we didn't. My mom drove. I saw lots of beautiful trees and flowers from the car, and I took lots of photos.

Jess That's nice! Were you with your brother?

Jacob No, my brother didn't come. He had a soccer game. I went there with my mom and dad.

Jess Was the climb fun?

Jacob Yes, it was fun! But it was dangerous, too. It started to rain when we were at the top. We were wet! I was scared, but my dad helped me to hike down.

Jess Oh, no! So, how long did you hike for?

Jacob We hiked for four hours! Two hours to go up, and two hours to go down. I was tired at the end!

Jess Sure, that's a long walk!

Jacob Yes! Now my parents want to climb Treasure Mountain.

Jess Treasure Mountain is fantastic!

Jacob Yes, I know. But I'd like to climb Diamond Mountain.

Jess Wow! I don't know Diamond Mountain, but I'd like to climb it with you!

Jacob Of course!

Unit 1 page 18

 03

Security Guard Hello! And welcome to the Shield Museum.

Girl Thank you!

Security Guard OK. Before you go in, I have to tell you the rules at the museum.

Girl OK.

Security Guard First, you have to show your ticket to the woman at the door. Do you have your ticket?

Girl Yes, I do. Look.

Security Guard Good! Now, there are a lot of very old shields in the museum. Some are more than six hundred years old.

Girl Wow! That's amazing!

Security Guard You can look at the shields, but you aren't allowed to touch them. OK?

Girl OK. No touching, then. But can I take photos of the shields?

Security Guard Oh, I'm sorry, but you can't. You aren't allowed to take photos of the shields. But there are lots of postcards in the store. You can buy the ones that show your favorite shields. Ah! And I see that you're carrying a bag.

Girl Yes. Can I take my bag into the museum?

Security Guard No, I'm sorry … You have to leave your bag in a locker. You aren't allowed to carry bags inside the museum.

Girl Fine. I'd like to see some very famous shields. Are there any?

Security Guard Yes, of course! There are a lot of very interesting shields. Some famous kings used them in their fights!

Girl Great! Oh! One more question: what time does the museum close?

Security Guard The museum closes at five o'clock. You have lots of time. Enjoy your visit!

Girl Thanks!

 04

Hi! I'm Kasim. Guess what? Our class went to the Knight Museum yesterday. The museum was fantastic, but we had some problems at the beginning. First, we went to see the helmets. There were some amazing helmets on a shelf. I was with my friend William. William took one of the helmets and put it on! When the woman from the museum saw William, she came and told him, "Take that helmet off, please. You aren't allowed to touch the helmets, shields, or swords in this museum." When our teacher, Mr. Martin, saw the woman, he ran to talk to her. But the woman told him, "You aren't allowed to run in this museum!" She wasn't happy! Well, the rest of our visit was fine. We didn't touch things, didn't run, and didn't shout. Then, on the bus back to school, William said, "Sorry, Mr. Martin. I only wanted to be a knight." So Mr. Martin told William, "You can be a knight in the school play." But William wasn't happy. He loves knights, but he doesn't like acting!

Unit 2 page 26

 05

Hi! You know, I had a really nice weekend in the country. My parents and I went to a forest near our house. We walked on a long path through the forest. There were some beautiful trees and fall leaves! We walked near a town, but we didn't stop there. When we came out of the forest, we saw a big mountain in front of us. We wanted to see the view from the top, so we climbed up the mountain. The view was amazing! We could see everything: the fields, the forest, and the town. I took lots of photos! We walked down the mountain, and we were hungry, so we looked for a place to eat. We found a nice field and had our picnic there. When we finished our picnic, it started to rain! We ran to the town because the rain was heavy. In the town, we found a nice café, and we had some cake there. It was a great way to end our adventure!

 06

Leo	Milly, look at this photo of me playing soccer.
Milly	Oh! You're a really good soccer player, Leo! How old were you in the photo?
Leo	I was six. Now I can play tennis, too. But I couldn't play tennis when I was six.
Milly	I see. What other sports could you play when you were six?
Leo	Well, I could swim. I learned when I was five, with you!
Milly	That's right! I enjoyed our swimming lessons. They were fun! Hey, could you play the guitar then?
Leo	No, I couldn't. I started guitar lessons when I was seven. And I couldn't ride a bike! I only learned last summer! But I could ride a scooter. I loved riding my scooter!
Milly	Yes, I remember! And I was very good at jumping rope, but you couldn't jump rope.
Leo	True! I couldn't jump rope when I was six, and I can't jump rope now. It's difficult!
Milly	Haha! But you could fly a kite when you were six. And that's not easy!
Leo	That's right. When I was six, I was really good at flying kites. My dad taught me!

Unit 3 page 34

 07

Hi! I'm going to tell you about last Sunday. My friends and I were in danger! It all happened in the park near my house. I went there with my friends Leah and John. The trees in that park are really tall, and the tallest tree is next to a river. We climbed that tree and … we got to the top! It was raining, but we were having fun. Suddenly, the rain turned into a big storm. We looked down at the river. There was a flood! There was water everywhere! And there was a very strong wind! We were trying to climb down, but it was very difficult. We weren't feeling happy any more. Luckily, Leah had her phone, and she called her parents. But she also called 911. Later, our parents came, and a fire engine arrived, too. A firefighter put a tall ladder up against the tree. She climbed up and helped us to come down from the tree. It was exciting, but we were scared, too.

The firefighter told us, "Next time, check the weather before you climb a tree!"

 08

1	**Mary**	What were you doing yesterday at three o'clock, Theo?
	Theo	I was watching a movie called *Fire!* It was fantastic. What about you, Mary?
	Mary	I was reading a book.
2	**Boy**	Amy, did you see the TV show about floods? It was at four o'clock.
	Amy	No, I didn't. I was playing soccer!
	Boy	You should watch it online. It was really interesting.
3	**Ms. Parker**	You didn't come to school yesterday, Jamie. Why?
	Jamie	I wasn't feeling well, Ms. Parker.
	Ms. Parker	Oh, I'm sorry to hear that. Are you OK now?
	Jamie	Yes, I am! Thanks!
4	**Harry**	Eva, what were you doing yesterday afternoon? Were you playing on your new game console?
	Eva	No, I wasn't, Harry! I was doing the homework about emergency workers. Remember?
	Harry	Oh, no! I forgot to do the homework!
5	**Girl**	Freddie, what time were you having breakfast yesterday?
	Freddie	At 12 o'clock.
	Girl	At 12 o'clock? That's late! What were you doing before?
	Freddie	I was sleeping!
6	**Grandpa**	How was the beach this morning, Rosie?
	Rosie	Oh, it wasn't great, Grandpa.
	Grandpa	Really? Why?
	Rosie	Because it was raining. We went to a town near the beach. And it wasn't raining there!

Unit 4 page 42

 09

Woman	Good morning. How can I help you?
Samuel	Hello. Can I have two one-way tickets to Cambridge, please?
Woman	Yes, of course. Did you say two one-way tickets?
Samuel	Yes, that's right. One ticket is for me, and the other one is for my mom. She's buying a cup of coffee at the moment. She loves coffee!
Woman	Ah, I see!
Samuel	How much is that?
Woman	That's £9, please.
Samuel	£9. OK. Here you go.
Woman	Thank you. Here are your tickets. You need to go to Platform number 2.
Samuel	Thanks. Where's Platform 2?
Woman	Go up the escalator and over the bridge. The platform is right there.
Samuel	Great. Oh! What time does the next train leave?
Woman	Hmm … Let me see. The next train to Cambridge is … at 10. That's right, at 10 o'clock. You have a big backpack and a suitcase there. Do you need help?
Samuel	I'm OK, thanks! My mom is coming back from the café now.

 10

Every year, my dad and I go to the theater in London. That's one of the best days of the year. Last Saturday was "theater day" for me and Dad. At nine in the morning, we were at the station. We were very excited! We got our tickets to go to London. Then Dad bought a cup of tea, and he bought me an apple juice. Our train arrived at Platform 1, but Dad was worried. He was looking for our theater tickets, and he couldn't find them. We got on the train and found our seats. When the train left the station, Dad was looking really worried. "I don't have our tickets!" he said. We got to London and walked to the theater, but we were feeling sad. We didn't have tickets for the play! "Let's buy new tickets," Dad said. At the theater, lots of people were waiting in front of the ticket office. When it was our turn, Dad said to the man at the desk, "I had two tickets for today, but I think I lost them." "What's your name, sir?" said the man. "Jonathan Gray," said Dad. Then the man said, "I have your tickets here, Mr. Gray. You asked to pick them up at the theater. Here you are." That was a great surprise! Right then, Dad and I walked up the stairs to our seats. And we really enjoyed the play!

Unit 5 page 50

11

Boy	So, what happened yesterday, Kelly?
Kelly	Well, my mom and I were looking for a birthday present for my dad. We wanted to buy him a special pen and some nice notebooks. My dad's a journalist. He writes his stories on the computer now, but he used to have lots of notebooks, and he used to collect different pens.

Boy	Sounds nice! So, which store did you go to?
Kelly	Oh, we were in a pen store. It's new, and it's called Write Now. It used to be a clothing store. It's next to the sports center.
Boy	Oh! I think I know it.
Kelly	Well, when my mom and I were choosing a notebook, we saw a woman. She looked strange. She was putting some pens in her bag! And they were really expensive ones!
Boy	Oh, no!
Kelly	Yes! She was tall with long, blond hair, and she had a scar on her cheek.
Boy	Wow! So what did you do?
Kelly	My mom told the salesclerk. But by then, the woman wasn't in the store anymore. The salesclerk called the police. They came very quickly and asked us some questions.
Boy	Did they catch the woman?
Kelly	No, they didn't. But I hope that they do!
Boy	Your dad has to write a story about that!

Teacher	OK, Max, it's your turn. Tell us, what would you like to do when you're older?
Max	I'd like to be a police officer when I grow up. My aunt Vicky is a photographer now, but she used to be a police officer, and I want to be just like her. Auntie Vicky was a police officer for ten years. She was in danger many times, so she had to be careful. And she used to work all night! But my aunt liked doing her job and helping people. She had to wear a special navy blue uniform, and she had a cool walkie-talkie. I remember she used to carry it everywhere! My aunt also used to drive a police car to chase criminals. And she caught more than one! Look, this is a photo of Auntie Vicky as a police officer. She looked very different! Her hair used to be dark and straight, you see? It's blond and curly now!
Teacher	That's great, Max. I didn't know the story about your aunt. She can teach you to be the best police officer in town!

Unit 6 page 58

🎧 13

OK, children. Let's start the story. Once upon a time, there was a terrible beast. It lived in a cave, in a faraway forest. The beast had a long, black tail, and its tongue was yellow. The people from the town near the forest were very scared of that creature. They called it "the Terrible Omnix" and said to visitors, "You shouldn't go into the forest." The Terrible Omnix had big wings. Its neck was thick and long. And there were scales, lots of scales, on the beast's back. And on its head, there were three short horns. Some people said that the Omnix looked like a dragon. They said that it was the biggest dragon in the forest. One day, a girl from the town went into the forest. Her name was Maya. Would you like to listen to her story? Well …

🎧 14

Laura	Edward, can I see your book?
Edward	Yes, here you are, Laura.
Laura	*The Terrible Omnix*. It looks interesting.
Edward	It's great! It's about a girl named Maya. She goes into a forest and finds strange beasts and creatures there.
Laura	Why is the book called *The Terrible Omnix*?
Edward	Well, the Omnix is the biggest and most dangerous beast in the forest. He looks like a dragon. But there are other creatures, too. First, Maya finds a small beast, and she calls it the Munkle. Then she meets two creatures that look like crocodiles, and she calls them the Trussock and the Arkle. The Trussock and the Arkle are bigger than the Munkle. The Munkle is the smallest beast in the forest, and it looks like a monkey.
Laura	Wow! Can I look at these beasts? I like their names. They're funny!
Edward	Yes, sure! Look, here they are. They're really cool, but my favorite beast is called the Galloping Runnyback.
Laura	The Galloping Runnyback? What does that one look like? Can I see?
Edward	Sure! Here it is. It looks like a horse, you see? I think its wings are fantastic! The Galloping Runnyback is the most beautiful creature in the forest. It's more beautiful than the Ginocat. And it's faster, too. But the fastest beast is the Gagger. The Gagger looks like a dinosaur!
Laura	Like which dinosaur? Like a stegosaurus?
Edward	No. The Gagger looks like a T-Rex.
Laura	Wow! It's a great book, Edward. Can I read it when you finish it?
Edward	Of course!

Unit 7 page 66

🎧 15

1	**Girl**	Is the purple guitar yours, Henry?
	Henry	No, it isn't. That's Jake's. And Sam's is the orange one.
	Girl	Is the black guitar yours, then?
	Henry	Yes, my guitar is the black one.
2	**Boy**	Is this yellow tambourine yours, Kate?
	Kate	No, it isn't. It's Tom's.
	Boy	Are you sure it's his?
	Kate	Yes, I am. Tom plays his yellow tambourine every day.
	Boy	OK. So is the brown tambourine yours?
	Kate	No, mine is the white tambourine. I don't like brown!
3	**Man**	Lily, would you like to play the trumpet?
	Lily	Hmm … I'm not sure about the trumpet. Can I play the violin?
	Man	Hmm … I need someone for the drums. Do you like the drums?
	Lily	Yes, I do! OK, I can play the drums.
	Man	Great! Thanks, Lily.
4	**Girl**	OK, here is my red keyboard. Now, is the green keyboard yours, Tony?
	Tony	No, it isn't mine. The green keyboard is Carmen's.
	Girl	OK. So this blue keyboard is …
	Tony	Mine!
	Girl	Oh! I like your blue keyboard, Tony!
5	**Ronnie**	Do you play a musical instrument, Ruby?
	Ruby	Yes, I do. Guess!
	Ronnie	Hmm … You play the guitar!
	Ruby	No! I play the piano. What about you, Ronnie?
	Ronnie	I play the recorder. But I think the piano is more exciting!

1 Girl Look! That's the school where Oliver goes.

Boy Really?

Girl Yes. It's a special music school. They learn to play different musical instruments.

Boy That's great!

2 Girl Is this the theater where Ivy played in the orchestra?

Boy Yes, that's right. It's called the Archway Theater.

3 Girl Where are you going, Tim?

Tim I'm going to see Ava.

Girl Who's Ava?

Tim Ava is the girl who sang at the party last night. Do you remember?

Girl Oh, yes! She's a great singer!

4 Boy OK, Amelia. Look, all these instruments are ours.

Amelia Ours?

Boy Well, they are the school's, but we can play them.

Amelia Any of them? I'd like to play the harp!

5 Girl Is that instrument yours, Lucas?

Lucas No, it isn't. That's my sister's. But look, the instrument that I play is over there. On the desk.

Girl Wow! Do you play the keyboard?

Lucas Yes, I do! Do you want to try it?

Unit 8 page 74

I'm Robert, one of the astronauts on the Moon X27 mission. We are back on our planet safely now, and it was all thanks to Rachel. Rachel is the newest astronaut on my team. And Moon X27 was her first mission. So, two weeks ago we were on the moon. Our rocket wasn't working, and we didn't know how to fix it. And our communications system was working really badly, so we couldn't talk to the astronauts on the space station. We needed help. And we needed it quickly! Then Rachel had an idea. She started to press some buttons and make some notes. After some time, Rachel said, "I think the rocket will work again." I listened carefully. Rachel said, "First, you press this. Then you move that very slowly. After that, you test this part of the rocket. Finally, you turn this on. Now, the screen should go blue …" And the screen went blue! The rocket was working again, and we could go home happily!

Interviewer Hello, and welcome back to Earth, Rachel!

Rachel Thank you.

Interviewer You're a very famous astronaut now. You helped fix the Moon X27 rocket!

Rachel Well, thanks! I had the idea, but we all worked hard together to come back home!

Interviewer That's amazing. So, what will you and your team do next?

Rachel Well, I think we'll look carefully at the Moon X27 rocket. We want to know why the rocket stopped working. All space missions have to be safe for astronauts.

Interviewer Sure. And will you go to the moon again?

Rachel Yes, I will. But I think my next mission will be on Mars.

Interviewer Will you travel to Mars?

Rachel Yes, I think that will be next year. The mission is called Mars X14. I'll go with some astronauts from the Moon X27 mission.

Interviewer That sounds exciting! Good luck, and thank you for talking to us, Rachel.

Unit 9 page 82

Jake We're going to the campsite tomorrow, Mom!

Mom I know! We'll have a great time, Jake.

Jake I want to dive into the lake and swim to the other side.

Mom Great! I'll dive into the lake with you.

Jake Nice! And can we make a fire?

Mom Yes, we can collect wood and make a fire.

Jake That will be cool! Can we sail a boat, too?

Mom Well, we can sail a boat, or we can make a raft.

Jake Wow! OK, I don't want to sail a boat. I want to make a raft!

Mom OK. Let's make a raft! Look, Jake, it says here that you can swing on a rope at the campsite. Would you like to do that?

Jake Hmm … No, thanks Mom. I don't like swinging on ropes.

Mom OK. Hmm …

Jake What are you thinking, Mom?

Mom You can wash and dry your clothes at the campsite.

Jake Oh, Mom! No! I don't want to wash or dry clothes!

Mom Haha! No problem, Jake. You don't have to do that. But you can help to put up the tent.

Jake That's exciting, Mom! I'll put up the tent with you and Dad.

Dad OK, Suzie. Let's pack the food and drinks for our camping trip.

Suzie OK, Dad!

Dad How many bottles of water do we have? Can you look in the fridge?

Suzie OK. We have … two, three, four … five. Five bottles of water.

Dad Great! Now, the bread is in that box. Are there two loaves?

Suzie Let me see … We have three loaves of bread, Dad. And there are some cans of soup. Let me count them. One, two … five, six; there are six cans of soup.

Dad That's good. Is there any rice in the box?

Suzie Oh, yes, Dad. Here it is. We have one bag of rice.

Dad OK, that's great.

Suzie Dad, can we take some bananas?

Dad Of course! Let's take some bananas. And we can buy some apples at the campsite.

Suzie OK. And what about some chocolate?

Dad Good idea. Let's take two small bars of chocolate. One bar for you and the other one for me, OK? There aren't any big bars.

Suzie Mmm! That's nice, Dad!

Acknowledgments

The authors and publishers acknowledge the following sources of copyright material and are grateful for the permissions granted. While every effort has been made, it has not always been possible to identify the sources of all the material used, or to trace all copyright holders. If any omissions are brought to our notice, we will be happy to include the appropriate acknowledgments on reprinting and in the next update to the digital edition, as applicable.

Key: ST = Starter, U = Unit

Photography

The following images are sourced from Getty Images.

ST: Tetra Images; Juanmonino/iStock/Getty Images Plus; Robert Niedring/Alloy; ViewStock; Artur Debat/Moment; Robert Niedring/MITO images; Rainer Dittrich; Sebastian Condrea/Moment; Westend61; **U1:** skodonnell/E+; Ng Sok Lian/EyeEm; bob_sato_1973/iStock/Getty Images Plus; MikeyGen73/iStock/Getty Images Plus; Sean Gladwell/Moment; dja65/iStock/Getty Images Plus; Donald Iain Smith/Blend Images; charlybutcher/iStock/Getty Images Plus; RMAX/iStock/Getty Images Plus; Westend61; Lorenzo Dominguez/Moment; Lee Harris/EyeEm; **U2:** Imgorthand/E+; Mint Images/Mint Images RF; Stephen Dorey/The Image Bank; GCShutter/E+; kali9/E+; Erika Fournier/EyeEm; Martin Ruegner/The Image Bank; **U3:** PaulJRobinson/iStock/Getty Images Plus; Marizza/iStock/Getty Images Plus; Merethe Svarstad Eeg/EyeEm; hsvrs/iStock/Getty Images Plus; Thinkstock/Stockbyte; ChrisCrafter/E+; **U4:** Madhourse/iStock/Getty Images Plus; Bim/iStock/Getty Images Plus; Chris Mellor/Lonely Planet Images/Getty Images Plus; MonicaNinker/iStock/Getty Images Plus; **U5:** aijohn784/iStock/Getty Images Plus; lillisphotography/E+; Oppenheim Bernhard/Stone/Getty Images Plus; **U6:** Alphotographic/iStock/Getty Images Plus; Danita Delimont/Gallo Images/Getty Images Plus; **U7:** C Squared Studios/Photodisc; Francesco Milanese/iStock/Getty Images Plus; Trodler/iStock/Getty Images Plus; bevrnja/iStock/Getty Images Plus; Hogie/iStock/Getty Images Plus; mrdoggs/iStock/Getty Images Plus; **U8:** Maike Hildebrandt/iStock/Getty Images Plus; KrisCole/iStock/Getty Images Plus; 1971yes/iStock/Getty Images Plus; Nick White/DigitalVision; **U9:** miljko/E+; Jamie Grill/Photodisc; Anton Petrus/Moment.

The following image is sourced from another library.

U1: Andrey Kuzmin/Alamy Stock Photo.

Illustrations

A Corazon Abierto (Sylvie Poggio Artists); Clive Goodyer (Beehive Illustration); Anna Hancock (Beehive Illustration); Marek Jagucki; Chris Lensch; Alex Patrick (Bright Group); Alan Rowe (Beehive Illustration); David Sem; Dave Smith (Beehive Illustration).

Audio

Audio production by John Marshall Media.

Typeset

EMC Design Limited.

Cover design by We Are Bold.

Packager

Integra